CROATIAN-ENGLISH
ENGLISH-CROATIAN

DICTIONARY AND PHRASEBOOK

T0275283

CROATIAN-ENGLISH
ENGLISH-CROATIAN

DICTIONARY AND PHRASEBOOK

Ante Antunović Šušnjar

Edited by

Eva Šušnjar-Hendricks

Hippocrene Books, Inc.
New York

For information, address:
HIPPOCRENE BOOKS, INC.
171 Madison Avenue
New York, NY 10016

Library of Congress Cataloging-in-Publication Data

Antunovic Susnjar, Ante.
    Croatian-English, English-Croatian : dictionary
and phrasebook / Ante Antunovic Susnjar ; edited
by Eva Susnjar-Hendricks.
        p. cm.
    ISBN 0-7818-0810-3
    1. Croatian language--Dictionaries--English.
    2. English language--Dictionaries--Croatian.
    I. Susnjar-Hendricks, Eva. II. Title.

PG1377 .A65 2000
491.8'2321--dc21

                                        00-058125

CONTENTS

ABBREVIATIONS

adj.	adjective
f.	feminine
for.	formal
infor.	informal
m.	masculine
n.	noun
nt.	neuter
pl.	plural
sing.	singular
v.	verb

THE CROATIAN ALPHABET
AND PRONUNCIATION
(HRVATSKA ABECEDA I IZGOVAR)

The Croatian language is phonetic. It consists of 30 sounds and 30 letters. Each letter corresponds to a sound. The Croatian alphabet does not include the letters q, w, x, or y. These letters only appear in foreign words.

Hard consonants: d, g, h, l, n, t.
Soft consonants: c, ć, č, d, đ, dž, j, lj, nj, š, ž.
Consonants that can be both hard and soft: b, f, k, m, p, r, s, v, z.

Letters	Pronunciation	Approximate English Equivalent
A a	a	c**ar**
B b	b	**b**ig
C c	ts	fi**ts**
Ć ć	ch	**ch**at
Č č	chu (harder than ć)	**ch**urch
D d	d	**d**o
Đ đ	gi	**g**inger
DŽ dž	dzh	**j**umbo
E e	eh	**e**ver
F f	f	**f**ather
G g	g	**g**ood
H h	h	**h**appy
I i	long e	b**ee**

J j	y	**y**ou
K k	k	**k**ite
L l	l	**l**ove
Lj lj	leh-ya	mi**lli**on
M m	m	**m**other
N n	n	**n**o
Nj nj	neh'ya	o**ni**on
O o	o	sn**o**w
P p	p	**p**uff
R r	r (rolled)	**r**ight
S s	s	**s**on
Š š	sh	**sh**ed
T t	t	**t**able
U u	oo	sh**oe**
V v	v	**v**ault
Z z	z	**z**ero
Ž ž	zh	televi**si**on

ACCENTED VOWELS

Letters	Examples	Accent
A â	pâs / belt	(long)
Á á	pás / dog	(short)
Ê ê	rare	(long)
É é	rare	(short)
Û û	ûžé / rope	(long)
Ú ú	úže / narrower	(short)
Î î	bîlo / it was	(long)
Í í	bílo / pulse	(short)

A VERY BASIC GRAMMAR

NOUNS

Croatian nouns have three genders: masculine, feminine, and neuter.

Masculine nouns end in a consonant, for example: *muž* (man), *otac* (father), *dječak* (boy), *pas* (dog).

The feminine nouns end in *-a*. For example: *žena* (woman), *sestra* (sister), *mama* (mother), *mačka* (cat), *stolica* (chair). The exceptions to this rule are nouns that end in a consonant but are feminine, for example, *stvar* (thing), *kost* (bone), *buducnost* (future), *jesen* (fall or autumn), *prošlost* (past).

The neuter nouns end in the vowels *-o* or *-e*. For example: *drvo* (tree), *slovo* (letter), *more* (sea), *polje* (field), *pile* (chick).

The plural of animate masculine nouns is formed by adding *-i*, *-evi*, or *-ovi*. For example: *mlinovi* (mills), *očevi* (fathers), *muževi* (men), *volovi* (oxen). The masculine inanimate nouns with hard endings end in *-ovi*, for example: *stolovi* (tables). Masculine inanimate nouns with soft endings will end in *-evi*, for example: *strojevi* (machines), *krajevi* (countryside).

Feminine plural nouns end in *-e*, for example: *žene* (women), *sestre* (sisters), *mame* (mothers), *mačke* (cats), *stolice* (chairs). However, if the nouns have consonant endings, they will end in *-i*. For example: *kosti* (bones), *stvari* (things), *kokosi* (hens).

Singular neuter nouns end in *-o* or *-e*. If they end in *-o*, then in the plural they will end in *-a*. For example: *auto* (car) will change to *auta* (cars). If they end in *-e*, then in the plural they will end in *-ići*. For example: *pile* (chick) will change to *pilići* (chicks). There are several exceptions to this rule, for example, *tele* (calf) will change to *telad* (calves), and *prase* (piglet) will change to *prasad* (piglets).

PRONOUNS

I	*ja*
you	*ti* (singular and/or informal)
he	*on*
she	*ona*
it	*ono*
we	*mi*
you	*vi* (plural and/or formal)
they	*oni* (m.)
they	*one* (f.)

The formal *vi* is used when addressing a stranger, a person you do not know very well, or a person of authority. This formal version of "you", *vi*, shows respect and distance. The informal version of "you", *ti*, is used to address family and good friends. It shows friendliness, closeness, and familiarity.

POSSESSIVE PRONOUNS

	(m.)	(f.)	(nt.)	(pl.)
my	*moj*	*moja*	*moje*	*moji*
your	*tvoj*	*tvoja*	*tvoje*	*tvoji*
his	*njegov*	*njegova*	*njegovo*	*njegovi*
her	*njen*	*njena*	*njenzino*	*njezini*
our	*naš*	*naša*	*naše*	*naši*
your	*vaš*	*vaša*	*vaše*	*vaši*
their	*njihov*	*njihova*	*njihovo*	*njihovi*

ADJECTIVES

Adjectives have three genders. The masculine singular usually ends with a consonant — *dobar* (good), *liep* (pretty), *jak* (strong). The feminine singular will end in -*a*. For example: *dobra* (good), *liepa* (pretty), *milá* (kind). The neuter singular ends in -*o*. For example: *dobro* (good), *liepo* (pretty), *milo* (kind).

The masculine plurals end in -*i*. For example: *dobri* (good), *liepi* (pretty), *mili* (kind). The feminine plurals end in -*e*. For example: *dobre* (good), *liepe* (pretty), *mile* (kind). Neuter plurals end in -*a*. For example: *dobrâ* (good), *liepâ* (pretty), *milâ* (kind).

ADVERBS

To create adverbs in Croatian, you add the suffix -*o* or -*e*. For example: *milo* (kindly), *zdravo* (healthy), *drago* (dearly).

COMPARISONS

Comparisons are formed from adjectives by adding the suffix *-ji* (masculine), *-ja* (feminine), and *-je* (neuter). The superior form is created by adding the prefix *-naj*.

	(m.)	(f.)	(nt.)
kind	*mio*	*mila*	*milo*
kinder	*miliji*	*milija*	*milije*
kindest	*najmiliji*	*najmilija*	*najmilije*

Exceptions are:

	(m.)			(m.)
good	*dobar*		bad	*zao*
better	*bolji*	and	worse	*gori*
best	*najboli*		worst	*najgori*

VERBS

The Present Tense - *(Regular Verbs)*
The present tense is formed by deleting the ending *-ti* from the infinitive and adding *-m* for the first person singular (personal pronoun *ja*). For the second person singular (*ti*), *-š* is added. For the third person singular (*on, ona,* and *ono*), the *-ti* is dropped from the infinitive, but no additional suffix is added. The ending *-mo* is used for the first person plural (*mi*). For the second person plural (*vi*), *-te* is added. And, for the third person plural *oni*, *-ju* is added.

Pronoun	Suffix
ja	-m
ti	-š
on	—
ona	—
ono	—
mi	-mo
vi	-te
oni	-ju

The Past Tense

The past tense is formed by deleting the ending -*ti* from the infinitive and adding endings -*o* (m.), -*la* (f.), or -*lo* (nt.) in singular and -*li* in plural (*mi, vi, oni*). For example, to change *dati* (to give) from present to past tense, take the verb stem *da* and add -*o* for masculine, -*la* for feminine, -*lo* for neuter and -*li* (m.), -*le* (f.), and -*la* (nt.) for plural. For example: *dao, dala, dalo, dali* (gave); *brao, brala, bralo, brali* (picked).

Pronoun	m.	f.	nt.
ja	-o	-la	-lo
ti	-o	-la	-lo
on	-o	—	—
ona	—	-la	—
ono	—	—	-lo
mi	-li	-le	-la
vi	-li	-le	-la
oni	-li	-le	-la

The Future Tense

The future tense is formed with the auxiliary *budem, budeš, bude, budemo, budete, budu*, and the infinitive of the verb. Only the first verb is conjugated, while the second must be in the infinitive form, for example:

Ja budem čitati.	I will read.
Ti budeš čitati.	You will read.
On bude čitati.	He will read.
Ona bude čitati.	She will read.
Mi budemo čitati.	We will read.
Vi budete čitati.	You will read.
Oni budu čitati.	They will read.

Reflexive Verbs

Some verbs have the suffix *-se*. This ending indicates a reflexive verb, like *prati se* (to wash oneself) as opposed to *prati* (to wash, somebody or something).

Present Tense Conjugation of Croatian Verbs

BITI — TO BE

	(s.)	(pl.)
1st	ja sam	mi smo
2nd	ti si	vi ste
3rd m.	on je	oni su
3rd f.	ona je	one su
3rd nt.	ono je	ona su

IMATI — TO HAVE

	(s.)	(pl.)
1st	ja imam	mi imamo
2nd	ti imaš	vi imate
3rd m.	on ima	oni imaju
3rd f.	ona ima	one imaju
3rd nt.	ono ima	ona imaju

HTJETI — TO WANT

	(s.)	(pl.)
1st	ja hoću	mi hoćemo
2nd	ti hoćeš	vi hoćete
3rd m.	on hoće	oni hoće
3rd f.	ona hoće	one hoće
3rd nt.	ono hoće	ona hoće

IĆI — TO GO

	(s.)	(pl.)
1st	ja idem	mi idemo
2nd	ti ideš	vi idete
3rd m.	on ide	oni idu
3rd f.	ona ide	one idu
3rd nt.	ono ide	ona idu

ŽIVJETI — TO LIVE

	(s.)	(pl.)
1st	ja živem	mi živemo
2nd	ti živeš	vi ževete
3rd m.	on žive	oni žive
3rd f.	ona žive	one žive
3rd nt.	ono žive	ona žive

ZNATI — TO KNOW

	(s.)	(pl.)
1st	ja znam	mi znamo
2nd	ti znaš	vi znate
3rd m.	on zna	oni znaju
3rd f.	ona zna	one znaju
3rd nt.	ono zna	ona znaju

CROATIAN-ENGLISH DICTIONARY

A

a and; but
adresa address *n.*
aerodrom airport
Afrika Africa
ajme alas
akcija share (stock)
ako if
alkohol alcohol
alkoholičar alcoholic
ambulanta ambulance
ambulanta outpatient department
Američki American
Amerika America
Amerikanac American man
Amerikanka American woman
ananas pineapple
apoteka drugstore
arterija artery
atletika track and field
Austrija Austria
auto car
autobus bus
autobusna stanica bus stop
Azija Asia

B

baba; baka grandmother
babica midwife
baciti throw *v.*
bačva barrel
Badnja večer Christmas Eve
bakalar cod (fish)
balet ballet
balkon balcony
banana banana
banka bank
bazen za kupanje swimming pool
benzin gasoline
besmislica nonsense
bez without
bez dvojbe no doubt
beznadan desperate
bezsmrtan immortal
bezstidan shameless
bicikl bicycle
bik bull
biljka plant
bîlo gdje wherever
bîlo kad anytime; whenever
bîlo kako however
bîlo koji whichever; either
bîlo što whatever
bîlo tko anyone; whoever
biologija biology
bit u pravu be right
biti budan be awake
biti potreban be of use

biti pozvan be called
biti tužan be sad
biti be *v.*
biži peas
bjelac white man
bjelo white
blagajnik cashier
blagosloviti bless *v.*
blagovanje dining
blagovaona dining room
blato mud
blaženstvo bliss
blijed pale
blistati shine
blizak adjoining
blizanci twins
blizu near
bluza blouse
Bog God
bógat rich
boj battle *n.*
bóját se be afraid
bôjá color
bôjanje painting
bôjati color *v.*
bojevnik soldier
bólest disease; illness
bolestan sick
bolji better
bolnica hospital
bolničarka nurse
bolovi pain
bonboni candy

bor pine tree
bora wrinkle *n.*
Božić Christmas
bradat bearded
braniti defend *v.*
brašno flour
brat brother
brati pick *v.*
brdo mountain
breskva peach
brigati se worry *v.*
brijeg hill
brinuti se look after
brkovi mustache
brod boat
broj number
brojiti count *v.*
bronza bronze
brz quick
brže fester
brzi vlak express train
brzina speed *n.*
brzo quickly
brzoglas telephone
bubanj drum
bubreg kidney
bučan noisy
budala fool *n.*
budućnost future
bufet buffet
bunar well (water)
but thigh

C

carina customs
celer celery
centar center
cesta road
Ciganin Gypsy
cigareta cigarette
cikla beet
cilj goal
cimet cinnamon
cink zinc
cipela shoe
cirkus circus
cjeli whole
cjena price *n.*
cjeniti value *v.*
cjenjeni esteemed
crijeva intestines
crkva church
crn black
crnac black man
crven red
cvijet flower
cvjetača cauliflower

Ć

ćelav bald
ćelija cell
ćirilica cyrillic alphabet
ćosav beardless

ćošak corner
ćud temper

Č

čačkalica toothpick
čaj tea
čarape socks
časopis magazine
čast honor *n.*
častna sestra nun
častoljubiv ambitious
Čeh Czech
ček check
čekati wait *v.*
čelni first
čelo forehead
čep plug
čep (od plutva) cork
češalj comb *n.*
Česka Republika Czech Republic
češljat kosu comb one's hair
češljati comb *v.*
češnjak garlic
čestitati congratulate
čestitke congratulations
čestitost virtue
često often
četka brush
četka za zube toothbrush
četverouglast square
četvrt quarter

četvrtak Thursday
čija (f.) whose
čiji (m.) whose
čije (nt.) whose
čin act *n.*
činovnik clerk
čir ulcer
čišćenje cleaning
čist clean *n.*
čistit clean *v.*
čistoća cleanliness
čitanje reading
čitati read
član member
članak article
čokolada chocolate
čovjek man
čudan strange
čuđenje wonder
čuti hear
čuvati guard *v.*
čvrst firm

D

da yes
daleko far
dalje away; further
dan (dobar dan) day (good day)
danas today
dar gift
darežljivost generosity

darovati present *v.*
dati give
datum date
davno long ago
debela (f.) fat
debeo (m.) fat
debelo (nt.) fat
deka blanket
deset ten
deseti tenth
devedeset ninety
devet nine
deveti ninth
devetnaest nineteenth
dim smoke *n.*
dimiti smoke *v.*
dinja watermelon
dio part *n.*
disati breathe
diviti se admire
divlji wild
djeca children
dječak boy
djed grandfather
djelovanje action
djete baby; child
djever (husband's brother) brother-in-law
djevojka girl
dlakav hairy
dlan palm
dnevna soba living room
dno bottom
do near

do njega next to
do viđenja good-bye
doba time (era)
dobit get
dobro good
dobro došli welcome
dobrota kindness
doći come
doći na vrijeme arrive on time
doći zrakoplovom arrive by air
dodatni additional
događaj occurrence
dohvatit get
dojam impression
dojka breast
dokaz proof
dokazati prove
doktor doctor
doktorat doctorate
dolar dollar
dolazak arrival
doli down; below
dolina valley
domaćinstvo household
domorodac native
donijeti bring
donji lower
doplatiti pay extra
dopremit carry (by vehicle)
dopunjujući supplementary
doputovati arrive
doručak breakfast
dosadan boring

dosadan posao tedious work
dosljedan strict
dosta enough
dosta vremena enough time
dovršiti complete; finish
dovršiti end *v.*
dozvola permission
dozvoliti allow; let
draga darling
draga (f.) dear
dragi (m.) dear
dragovoljac volunteer
drhtati shiver *v.*
droga drug
drugi second *adj.*
drugi put next times
drugom prilikom at other times
društveni public
društvo society
drvo wood
držati hold *v.*
država country; state
dûb oak
dubok deep
dûg debt
dúgá (f.) long
dúg (m.) long
dúgo (nt.) long
dûgá rainbow
dugme button
dúh spirit
dûša soul

dúševni spiritual
dužina length
dúzina dozen
dužnost duty
dva two
dvadeset twenty
dvanaest twelve
dvanaesti twelfth
dvojica couple
dvopek toasted bread
dvorana hall

Đ

đak pupil
đačko doba school years
đački dom dormitory
đemper sweater
đon sole of shoe
đubar manure
đubrivo fertilizer
đubriti fertilize *v.*
đurdica white wildflower

DŽ

džamija mosque
džep pocket
džepni sat pocket watch

džin giant; gin
džungla jungle

E

električna struja electricity
elektronika electronic
emigracija emigration
energičan energetic
Engleska England
Engleski English (language)
Engleskinja Englishwoman
Englez Englishman
Europa Europe

F

fermentacija fermentation
filharmonija symphony
filozofija philosophy
fizika physics
flaša bottle
fotelja couch
fotoaparat camera
fotografija photograph
Francuska France
francuski french *adj.*
Francuskinja Frenchwoman
Francuz Frenchman
fratar monk
frizerka (f.) hairdresser

frizer (m.) hairdresser
frizura hairdo

G

gađenje disgust *n.*
garancija guarantee
garaža garage
garderoba coatroom
gdje where
geslo slogan
gibak flexible
gibanje motion
gitara guitar
glad hunger *n.*
gladak smooth
gladan hungry
glas voice
glasan loud
glasati vote *v.*
glava head
glavni main
glavni kolodvor central station
glazba music
gledati look *v.*
gljiva mushroom
globa penalty
globus globe
gluh deaf
glumac actor
glumica actress
glup stupid

gnjev anger *n.*
gnjili rotten
go naked
godina year
godišnje yearly
godišnje doba season
godišnjica anniversary
górá mountain
gôrák bitter
góré up
górê worse
góriti burn *v.*
górivo fuel
gornji upper
gospođa Mrs.
gospođica Miss
gospodin Mr.
gost guest
gostiona restaurant
govedina beef
govor speech
góvôriti talk *v.*
gozba feast
grad town
građanin citizen
građevina building (under construction)
graditelj builder
graditi build
grah beans
gramofon record player
gramofonska ploča record (disk)
grana branch (tree)
granica border (between countries)

greška mistake *n.*
grijeh sin *n.*
griješiti sin *v.*
gripa flu
griz grits
grlo throat
grm bush
grmljavina thunder
grob grave
groblje cemetery
grozan terrible
grožde grape
groznica fever
grudi chest
gubljenje vremena waste of time
gulaš stew
guma za brisanje eraser
guska goose
gust dense
gvožde iron (metal)

H

haljina dress; skirt
haljine wardrobe
halo hello
himna anthem
hitni izlaz emergency exit
hlače trousers
hladno cold; cool
hodati walk *v.*
hodnik corridor

hokej hockey
hotel hotel
hrana food
hranjivost nourishment
hrast oak
hrđa rust *n.*
hrđat rust *v.*
hrkati snore *v.*
htjeti want *v.*
hvala thanks
hvalisati flatter *v.*
hvala praise *n.*
hvaliti praise *v.*

I

iako although
ići go *v.*
ići u grad go out
ideja idea
idući next
igla needle
igra game; play *n.*
igrač player
igračka toy
igrati se play *v.*
ikako at all
ili/ili either/or
imati have
ime name *n.*
imendan name's day
imenica noun

imenovanje nomination
imetak possession
inače otherwise
industrija industry
insekt bug
inžinjer engineer
isključiti disconnect
iskra spark
iskren sincere
iskustvo experience
ismijavati laugh at
ispasti fall out
ispit examination
ispiti drink up
isplatiti pay out
ispod down; below
ispod under
ispoljiti reveal
ispovjediti se confess in church
ispravan correct; proper
ispravka correction
ispred in front of
istina truth
istinito true
istočni eastern
istok east
istraga interrogation
istraga research *n.*
istraživati research *v.*
Italija Italy
iza behind
izabrati choose; elect
izazivati irritate

izbjeglica refugee
izbor choice
izbori election
izdajnik traitor
izdržati endure
izgled lica (boja) complexion
izgnanstvo exile
izgubiti lose
izgubljena (f.) to be lost
izgubljen (m.) to be lost
izgubljeno (nt.) to be lost
izići get out
izjesti finish eating
izlaz exit
izlaz u nuždi emergency exit
izlet excursion
izliječiti cure *v.*
izložba show; display *n.*
izložiti display *v.*
između between
izmjena exchange *n.*
izmjeniti exchange *v.*
iznad svega above all
iznenaditi surprise *v.*
izniman rare
iznimka exception
iznova start over
iznutra from inside
izseliti se move out
izučen trained
izumiti discover
izumrijeti become extinct

izuzetak exception
izuzetan exceptional
izvanredan wonderful
izvesti perform
izvratit turn out
izvrstan excellent
izvući pull out

J

ja I; me
jabuka apple
jadan miserable
jagoda berry; strawberry
jaje egg
jak strong (physically)
jámá cave; pit
jágnje lamb
jao alas
Japanac Japanese man
Japanka Japanese woman
jasan clear
jašenje riding
jašiti ride *v.*
jastučna navlaka pillowcase
jastuk cushion; pillow
jéčám barley
jedan (m.) one
jedan do drugog next to each other
jedan drugi another one
jedan sat hour
jedanaest eleven

jedanaesti eleventh
jedino only
jedna (f.) one
jednako equally
jedno (nt.) one
jednom once
jednostavan simple
jednostavno simply
jedriti sail *v.*
jedro sail *n.*
jedva hardly
jeftin cheap
jelo food
jer because
jesen autumn
jesti eat
jetra liver
jetrva sister-in-law
jezero lake
jezik language; tongue
još still; yet
jučer yesterday
jug south
juha broth; soup
jutro morning
južni southern

K

k, ka towards
kad; kada when
kafana café

kajsija apricot
kakao cocoa
kako how
kamata interest *v.*
kamen stone
Kanada Canada
kap drop *n.*
kaput coat; jacket
karakter character
karpet rug
karta map
kašalj cough *n.*
kašljat cough *v.*
kasnije later
kasno late
kat floor (story)
Katolik Catholic
kava coffee
kazalište theater
kazna punishment
kći daughter
keksi cookies
keramika ceramic
kesten chestnut
kilo kilogram
Kinez Chinese
kino cinema; movie
kip statue
kirurg surgeon
kiša rain *n.*
kiseo sour
kišiti rain *v.*
kišobran umbrella

kit whale
klavir piano
klicati cheer *v.*
klin wage
ključ key
klûpa bench
knedla dumpling
knjiga book
knjigovođa accountant
knjigovodstvo bookkeeping
književnost literature
knjižnica library
književnik writer
kobasica sausage
kočnica brake
kod at
kod kuće at home
kod tvoje kuće at your house
kofein caffeine
kofer suitcase
koje vrste what kind
koji which
koliko how many
koliko košta how much
koljeno knee
kolovoz August
komad piece
komarac mosquito
komedijaš clown
komputer computer
konačno finally
koncert concert

konj horse
konobar waiter
konobarica waitress
kontrolirati control *v.*
konzerva canned food
kopno land
kora bark *n.*
korak step
korist profit *n.*
koristiti utilize
kosa hair
košarka basketball
kost bone
košulja shirt
košuta doe
kotač wheel
kotlić saucepan
kovani novac change; money (coins)
koža skin
kozmički cosmic
krađa theft
krajnji extreme
krastavac cucumber
kratak short
kratkotrajan brief
kravata necktie; tie
krckavo crunchy
krčma wine tavern
kreda chalk
kredit credit
krema cream
krevet bed

krhki fragile
krilo wing
kristal mineral (stone)
krompir potato
krov roof
kroz through
krug circle
kruh bread
kruna crown
kruška pear
krv blood
krzneni kaput fur coat
kuća home; house
kućanica housewife
kucati knock *v.*
kuhanje cooking
kuhar cook *n.*
kuhati cook *v.*
kuhinja kitchen
kuka hook
kukac insect
kukuruz corn
kupac customer
kupaći kostim swimsuit
kupaona bathroom
kupanje bathing
kupati se bathe *v.*
kupiti buy
kupnja purchase *n.*
kupovati shop *v.*
kupus cabbage
kuraž courage

kut corner
kutija box
kvalitet quality
kvar flaw
kvasina vinegar

L

lahor breeze
lakat elbow
lako easy; light
lakouman frivolous
laku noć good night
lani last year
lav lion
lažan false
leća lentil
leći na lie down on
led ice
leđa back
lekcija lesson
leptir butterfly
letiti fly *v.*
ležati lying down
lice face *n.*
lift elevator
liječenje cure
liječiti treat *v.*
liječnik doctor
lijek medicine
lijen (m.) lazy

lijena (f.) lazy
lijeno (nt.) lazy
lijepa (m., f.) pretty
lijevi left
limun lemon
linija line
lipanj June
listopad October
lom crash *n.*
lopov robber
lopta ball
loša navika bad habit
losos salmon
lovac hunter
lubanja skull
lud crazy; insane
luđak madman
lúk onion
lûk arch; bow
lula pipe
lutati wander
lutka doll

Lj

ljekarna pharmacy
ljekarna drugstore
ljenost laziness
ljepilo glue *n.*
ljepiti glue *v.*
ljepota charm; beauty
ljepša (f.) more beautiful

ljepše (nt.) more beautiful
ljepši (m.) more beautiful
ljes coffin
lješnjak hazelnut
lješina carcass
ljettina harvest
ljetni of summer
ljeto summer
ljetos this summer
ljetošnji of this summer
ljetovanje summer vacation
ljevak funnel *n.*
ljiljan lily
ljubav love *n.*
ljubavnica (f.) lover
ljubavnik (m.) lover
ljubiti kiss *v.*
ljubljenje kissing
ljubomora jealousy
ljubica violet (flower)
ljubičasto violet (color)
ljudi men
ljudski human
ljudski rod mankind
ljudskost civility
ljukelj wild garlic
ljulj weed
ljuljačka swing *n.*
ljuljati se sway; swing *v.*
ljuska nutshell
ljutit angry; furious
ljutit se become angry
ljutnja anger *n.*

M

mačeha stepmother
mačka cat
Mađar Hungarian
madrac mattress
magarac donkey
magla fog
magnetofon tape recorder
majica tee shirt
majka; mama mother
majmun monkey
mak poppy
malen small
malinovac raspberry drink
malo little
mâna fault; flaw
mandarinka tangerine
manje less
manji smaller
marama kerchief
maramica handkerchief
marljiv diligent
mašina za pranje washing machine
maslo butter
mast grease; lard
matematika mathematics
materijal material
med honey
medeni mjesec honeymoon
medicina medicine
međunarodni international
medvjed bear

mekan (m.) soft
mekana (f.) soft
mekano (nt.) soft
melon melon
meni me
mermelada jam
merodije spice
meso meat
metar meter
metež bustle
mi I; me
mišica muscle
milost mercy
milosrđe compassion
milovati caress *v.*
mineralna vada mineral water
minuta minute
mir order; peace
miran calm
miris perfume
mirovina pension
miš mouse
misa mass (religious service)
misliti think
mišljenje opinion
mjera measure *n.*
mjeriti measure *v.*
mješati stir
mjesec moon
mjesec (dana) month
mjesni local
mjesto place *n.*
mlad young

mlâdâ bride
mlađi younger
mladić lad
mladost youth
mladoženja bridegroom
mlijeko milk
mnogo many; much
mnoštvo multitude
množenje multiplication
môć power
moći could
moda fashion
moderan modern
modrica bruise *n.*
moguć able
moguće probably
mogućnost possibility
moj (m.) mine
moja (f.) mine
moje (nt.) mine
mokar wet *adj.*
mokrača urine
molim please
moliti se pray
moral moral
morati must
more sea
morski pas shark
most bridge
motorcikl motorcycle
mozak brain
možda maybe; perhaps
mračan gloomy

mrak darkness
mraz frost
mrkva carrot
mrlja stain
mršav slim
mrtav dead
mrziti hate *v.*
mucati stutter
mučiti torture *v.*
mudar smart
mudrac wise man
muha fly *n.*
muzej museum

N

na on
na engleskom in English
na primjer for example
na silu by force
na vrijeme on time
na zdravlje to your health
nabaviti obtain
nabreknuti swell *v.*
načelnik director
naći find *v.*
nacija nation
nad above
nada hope *n.*
nadati se hope *v.*
nadimak nickname
nadkonobar head waiter

nadoknada compensation
nadoknaditi make up *v.*
nadzornik boss
nafta petroleum
nafta (nepročišćena) crude oil
nagomilati accumulate
najamnina rent *n.*
najbolji best
najčešće frequently
najgori worse
najmlađi youngest
najviše the most
nakazan deformed
nakit jewel
nalij fill up
namirnice food
namjera intention
namještaj furniture
nanoge on foot
naobrazba education
naočale eyeglasses
napad attack *n.*
napadati attack *v.*
napetost stress *n.*
napojnica gratuity
napokon finally; at last
napor effort
napraviti make
naprijed forward
napuni fill up
napustiti leave *v.*
naranča orange (fruit)
narančasta orange (color)

naravno of course
naredba command *n.*
narediti command *v.*
narod nation; people
narodna nošnja national costume
narodni national
naručiti order *v.*
narudžba order *n.*
naš (m.) our
naša (f.) our
naše (nt.) our
nasilje terror
naslaga deposit *n.*
nasljediti inherit
nasljedstvo inheritance
naučenjak scientist
nauka science
nauka o komputeru computer science
náviknût accustomed
nažalost unfortunately
ne no
ne razumjeti misunderstand
ne samo not only
nebo heaven
neboj se do not be afraid
nećakinja niece
nečistoća dirt
nedaleko nearby; not far
nedjelja Sunday
nedopadanje dislike *n.*
nedostaje be lacking
nedostatak shortage
nedozreo minor; unripe

negativan negative
negdje somewhere
negdje drugdje elsewhere
nego but
neizvjestan uncertain
neka vrsta some kind
neka; neka bude so be it
nekako somehow
neki some
neki drugi other
nekoliko several
nekoristan useless
nema nijedan there isn't any
neman monster
nemar neglect *n.*
nemir unrest
nemoralan immoral
nenadno sudden
neodgovoran irresponsible
neodlučan reluctant
neovisan independent
neposlušnost disobedience
nepošten dishonest
nepotrebno unnecessary
nepovjerenje mistrust
nepovjerljiv suspicious
nepoznat unknown
nepoznato foreign
nepravda wrong *n.*
nepravedan unjust; wrong *adj.*
nepravilan improper
neprijatelj enemy
nered mess

neredovit irregular
nesporazum misunderstanding
nesretan slučaj accident
nestati disappear; perish
nešto something
nestrpljiv impatient
nesvjest unconsciousness
netko someone
neudoban uncomfortable
neuspjeh failure
nevjerovatan unbelievable
nevjesta daughter-in-law
nezahvalnost ingratitude
nezakonit illegitimate; unlawful
nezanimljiv uninteresting
nezaposlen unemployed
nezdrav unhealthy
nezgoda mishap; misfortune
neženja bachelor
nezrelo not ripe
ni/niti neither/nor
nigdje nowhere
nijedan (m.) none
nijedna (f.) none
nijedno (nt.) none
nijem mute
nikad never
nisko low
ništa nothing
nitko nobody
niz row *n.*
noć night
noga leg

nogomet soccer
normalan normal
nos nose
nosač porter
noseća pregnant
nositi carry *v.*
nota musical note
novac currency; money
novčani financial
novela novel
novi new
novine newspaper
novost news
nož knife
nožice scissors
nula zero

NJ

njega him
njegov his
njegova hers
njegovo its
njegovati to care for
Njemac German man
Njemačka Germany
Njemački German language
Njemica German woman
njemu to him
njen (m.) hers
njena (f.) hers
njeno (nt.) hers

nježnost tenderness
njih them
njihov (m.) theirs
njihova (f.) theirs
njihovo (nt.) theirs
njiva planting field
njoj to her
nju her
njuh sense of smell
njušenje sniffing
njušiti sniff *v.*
njuška snout

O

obadva both
obala coast
obavezati se commit *v.*
obavještenje information
obazrivost caution
obećanje promise
običaj custom; fashion
običan ordinary; standard
obilan plentiful
obilje luxury
obitavalište residence
obitelj family
objesiti hang
oblačno cloudy
oblak cloud
oblast region
oblik figure

obojan colored
oboliti become ill
obor yard
obrađivati cultivate
obrana defense
obraz cheek
obrazložiti explain
obriti shave
obrtnik craftsman
obrva eyebrow
obučen dressed
obući se to get dressed
obziran tolerant
ocat vinegar
ocean ocean
očekivati expect
oćelaviti become bald
očevidno it is evident
oči u oči face-to-face
očni ljekar eye doctor
očuh stepfather
od from
od onda since then
od rane mladosti from an early age
odakle from where
odan devoted to
odavde from here
odbojka volleyball
odbor committee
odgovornost responsibility
odimljena riba smoked fish
odjeća clothing
odjeljenje department

odjelo suit
odkad from when
odlučan decisive
odlučiti decide
odluka decision
odmah at once
odmotati unfold
odnijeti take away
odozdol from below
odozgor from above
odputovati depart
odrasla osoba adult
odrasti to grow up
održavati maintain
odteći run off *v.*
oduševljen enthusiastic
odvratno disgusting
odvratnost disgust *n.*
oglas advertisement; notice
oglasna ploča bulletin board
ogledalo mirror *n.*
ogovaranje gossip *n.*
ograda fence *n.*
ogroman huge
ohladiti cool *v.*
ohol proud
ojačati strengthen
oko; oči (pl.) eye
oko/u about
okolnost situation
okolo around
okovratnik collar
okriviti accuse

okrug district
okrugao round
okružiti encircle
okus taste *n.*
olakšanje relief
olakšati make easier
olovka pencil
oluja storm
omogućiti make possible
omotak package
omotnica envelope
on he; him
ona she
onda then
oni they
općenito generally
opis description
opisati describe
opit se get drunk
opomena warning
oporuka last will
opozvati recall *v.*
oprostite mi excuse me
oprostiti forgive
opstanak livelihood
orah walnut
orao eagle
organizacija organization
orkan hurricane
orkestar orchestra; band
oružje weapon
oružnička postaja police station
oružnik policeman

osa wasp
osam eight
osamdeset eighty
osamnaest eighteen
osiguranje insurance
osigurati ensure
osim besides
osim toga besides that
osjećaj feeling
osjećati feel *v.*
osjetljiv sensitive
oslobođenje liberation
osoba person
osobina character
osobit special
osobna karta identity card
osobne isprave citizen ID
osobni private
osobno in person
ostatci leftovers
ostati remain; stay
oštrica tip (point)
ostriga oyster
osuda sentence *n.*
osuditi sentence *v.*
osušen dried
osveta revenge
osvjetlit light up
osvježiti refresh
osvježujuće piće refreshment
otac father
otimač robber
otok island

otrijeznit se become sober
otrov poison
otrovan poisonous
otvarač opener
otvoreno open *n.*
otvoriti open *v.*
ovaj put this time
ova (f.) this
ovaj (m.) this
ovako like this
ovan ram
ovca sheep
ovdje here
ovisiti depend
ovo (nt.) this
ovuda this way
ozbiljan serious
ozdravljenje recovery
oženjen (m.) married
ozlijeđen injured
ozljeda injury
ožujak March

P

pá dá of course
pacijent patient *n.*
pakao hell
pamćenje memory
papir paper
paprika paprika
par pair

para steam
parfem perfume
park park
parlamenat congress
pás dog
pâs belt
pas ovčar sheepdog
pasport passport
pasti fall *v.*
pasti doli fall down
pasti u nesvjest faint
pastrva trout
patka duck
patrola patrol
pauza intermission
pažnja interest *v.*
pčela bee
pečat stamp *n.*
pečen roasted
pečena govedina roast beef
peći bake
pecivo pastry
pedeset fifty
pedeseti fiftieth
pegla iron *n.*
peglati iron *v.*
pehar glass (tumbler)
pekar baker
penjati se climb
pepeljara ashtray
perad poultry
pero pen; feather
pet five

petak Friday
peti fifth
petnaest fifteen
petrusim parsley
piće drink *n.*
pijan drunk
pile chicken
pilot pilot *n.*
pingvin penguin
pisac writer
pisati write
pismo letter
pitanje question *n.*
pitati ask; inquire
piti drink *v.*
pivo beer
pješke on foot
pjesma poem; song
pjetao rooster
pjevati sing
plaća pay *n.*
plahta sheet
plakati cry *v.*
plan plan *n.*
planiranje planning
plata salary
platiti pay *v.*
plav blue
plaža beach
ples ball, gala
plesati dance *v.*
plesti knit *v.*
pletivo knitting

plitak shallow
plivati swim *v.*
pljeska slap *n.*
pljesnivo moldy
pljusak rain shower
pločnik sidewalk
plomba filling
pluća lungs
po after
pobjeda victory
pobjediti win *v.*
poboljšati improve
početak beginning
početi begin
počinak rest *n.*
počivati rest *v.*
pod floor
podići raise
podignut lift
podpis signature
podrignuti belch *v.*
podrum cellar
podupirati support *v.*
pogoditi metu hit (target)
pogoršati worsen
pogriješiti make a mistake
pohvala compliment
pojavit se appear
pojesti finish eating
pokazati show *v.*
pokisnuti get wet
pokojni deceased
pokopati bury

pokriti cover *v.*

pokrivač blanket *n.*

pokušati try

pokvariti spoil

pola half

pola kila half a kilo

poleđina backside

polje field

Poljska Poland

Poljski Polish

poljubac kiss *n.*

položiti put down

poluditi become insane

pomaknut move *v.*

pómôć help; aid *n.*

pomoći help *v.*

pomozi se help yourself

ponedjeljak Monday

ponekad sometime

poništiti cancel

ponoć midnight

ponos pride

ponoviti repeat *v.*

ponuda offer *n.*

ponuditi offer *v.*

poplašen startled

popodne afternoon

popraviti fix; repair

popržiti fry *v.*

porcija portion

pored besides

posađeno planted

posaditi plant *v.*

posao business
posebno especially
posjeta visit *n.*
posjetiti visit *v.*
poslati send
posljedica consequence
posljednji last
poslovan busy
poslovica proverb
poslušan obedient
poslužavnik tray
pošta post office
postaja station
postati become
postaviti place *v.*
postelja bed
poštivanje respect *n.*
poštivati respect *v.*
poštovan respectable
pósúde od gline crockery
posudit lend
poteškoća difficulty
potok stream
potražnja search *n.*
potreba necessity
potrebno necessary
potrošiti consume; spend
potrošnja consumption
potvrda certificate; receipt
povećati magnify *v.*
povijest history
povjerenje confidence
povjesni historical

povlašćen favorite
povod reason *n.*
povrće vegetable
površina surface
povući pull *v.*
požar fire (big)
pozdrav greeting
pozlaćen golden
poznanik acquaintance
poznat popular
požuri hurry *n.*
pozvati invite
prase; svinja pig
prasetina pork
prašina dust *n.*
prati (na ruke) wash (by hand)
pravac route
pravda justice
pravnik lawyer
právo straight
právo u straight in
právo do straight to
prazan empty *adj.*
praznici vacation *n.*
praznik holiday
preći preko cross *v.*
precizno precise
predaja tradition
predanost zeal
predgrađe suburb
predio territory
predmet subject
predpovjesni prehistoric

prehladit se catch a cold
prekjuče day before yesterday
prekosutra day after tomorrow
premda after all
premoren exhausted
preobradba restructuring
preokrenut turn over
preporučiti recommend
prepoznati recognize
prerađeno processed
prerezati cut *v.*
prestupak infraction
pretpostaviti suppose
prevara deception
prevariti deceive
prevod translation
prevodioc interpreter
prevoz transportation
prevoziti transport *v.*
pri at; near
priča story; tale
pričuvati watch over
prigovarati object *v.*
prigovor complaint
prijatan nice
prijatelj (m.) colleague; close friend
prijateljica (f.) colleague; close friend
prijava report *n.*
prijavit se enlist
prije podne late morning
prilagoditi suit *v.*
prilaz entrance
prilika chance; opportunity

primjetiti spot *v.*
pripraviti fix; prepare
pripreman ready *adj.*
pripremiti prepare
pripremljeno arranged
priroda nature
pristanak agreement
pristati agree
privlačan (m.) attractive
privlačna (f.) attractive
privlačno (nt.) attractive
privremeno temporarily
privržen devoted to
prizemlje first floor
priznanica receipt
priznati acknowledge
probaviti digest *v.*
problem problem
probuditi wake up
proći pass *v.*
prodaja sale
prodati sell *v.*
prodavač salesman
prodavačica saleswoman
prodavaona store
profesor professor
profinjen; delikatan delicate
proglas announcement
proglasiti announce
prognoza forecast *n.*
program program *n.*
progutati swallow *v.*
proizvesti produce *v.*

proizvod produce *n.*
proizvodnja production
prolaz passage; gate
proljeće spring
proljev diarrhea
promet traffic
promjeniti exchange; substitute
pronaći discover; locate
proplanak hillside
propuh draft *n.*
prosinac December
proširiti broaden
prosjak beggar
prosječan average
prošlost past
prosuti spill *v.*
protiv against
proždrijeti devour
prozirno transparent
prozor window
prst finger
prsten ring
pršut ham
prvi first
prženi fried
ptica bird
pucanje shooting
pucati shoot *v.*
pucki popcorn
puding pudding
pukotina fracture *n.*
puls pulse
pumpna stanica gas station

pun full
punac father-in-law (wife's father)
punica mother-in-law (wife's mother)
punjenje stuffing
punoljetant adult
pupak navel
puran turkey
purpuran purple
pušač smoker
pustolovina adventure
put road
putnički vlak passenger train
putovanje travel; trip
puzati crawl *v.*

R

rad work *n.*
radi dobro do well
radi toga therefore
radije rather
radinost industry
radio radio
radiona workshop
raditi do; work *v.*
radna soba workroom
radni dan workday
radnik worker
raj paradise
rajčica tomato
rak crab
rak rana cancer

rakija brandy
rame shoulder
rano early
rasipat waste *v.*
raskrsnica crossing
rasparati rip *v.*
raspoloženje mood
raspored schedule *n.*
rasprostranjen extensive
rastava divorce *n.*
rastaviti take apart
rastopiti dissolve
rat war *n.*
razbarušen disheveled
razdaljina distance *n.*
razdjeliti divide *v.*
razdražiti enrage
razglas broadcast *n.*
razglednica postcard
razgoljen striped
razgovarati converse
razgovor conversation
razlika difference
razmjena change *n.*
razmjeniti change *v.*
raznolik various
raznovrstan diverse
razočarati disappoint *v.*
razočaranje disappointment
razred class
razrušiti demolish
raširiti make wide
razum mind *n.*

razumjeti understand
razvod braka divorce
razvoj development
rebro rib
rečenica sentence (grammar)
reći say *v.*
remen belt
rentabilan profitable
reuma rheumatism
rezanci noodles
riba fish
ribizl currants
riža rice
rječ word
rječni rak crayfish
rječnik dictionary
rjeka river
rjetko seldom
roba široke potrošnje goods
robna kuća department store
robot robot
roda stork
róđak cousin; relative
rođendan birthday
rodit se be born
roditelj parent
roditi give birth
rotkvica radish
rub edge
ručak lunch *n.*
ručati to have lunch
ručni manual
ručni zglob wrist

rujan September
ruka arm; hand
rukav sleeve
rukavica glove
rupa hole
rupčić handkerchief
Rus Russian man
Ruskinja Russian woman
ruž lipstick
ruža rose
ružan ugly
ružičast pink

S

s; sa with
s mukom hardly
sa srećom fortunately
sabirač collector
saćut compassion
sád at once; now
sagrađen constructed
sákrit hidden
sakupljati gather
salama salami
salata salad
šalit se joke v.
salveta napkin
sam (m.) alone
sama (f.) alone
samljeti grind up
samo (nt.) alone

samoća solitude
samoposluga self-service
samostalan independent
samoubistvo suicide
samouvjerenje self-confidence
samovoz car
san dream *n.*
sanjati dream *v.*
sapun soap
sastanak meeting
sasvim completely
sat clock
saučešće condolence
sav whole
savjet advice
savjetovati advise
savršen perfect *n.*
sazvati summon *v.*
sebičan egoist
sedam seven
sedamdeset seventy
sedamnaest seventeen
sekunda second *n.*
seljak peasant
selo village
sendvić sandwich
sestra sister
sestrić nephew (sister's son)
sigurno surely
sigurnost safety
sila force *n.*
silovati rape *v.*
Silvestrovo New Year's Eve

sin son
sinovac nephew (brother's son)
sir cheese
siromah poor
siromaštvo poverty
sirota orphan
sirov raw
sitan small
sitniji smaller
sječanj January
sjed gray
sjediniti unite *v.*
Sjedinjene Države United States
sjediti sit *v.*
sjena shadow
sjevanje lightning
sjever north
sjeverni northern
skija ski *n.*
skijati se ski *v.*
skladatelj composer
skočit jump *v.*
skok jump *n.*
skorije sooner
skoro recently
skorup cream
skratiti shorten
skromnost modesty
skup gathering
skupina group
skupit se assemble; gather
skupo expensive
slab weak

slabost weakness
sladoled ice cream
slamka straw
slan salty
slanina bacon
slast zest
slatkiši sweets
slavan famous
slaviti celebrate
slezena spleen
sličan similar
slijediti follow
slika picture *n.*
sljedeći next
sloboda freedom
slobodan free
slobodouman freethinking
slomiti break *v.*
slon elephant
Slovačka Slovakia
slovkati spell *v.*
slučaj case *n.*
slušaoci audience
služba service
služiti serve
smanjiti make smaller
smeće dirt
smeđ brown
smetište garbage dump
smijati se smile *v.*
smiri se calm down
smjelost courage; bravery
smjer direction

smješán funny
smješati mix *v.*
smrditi stink *v.*
smrt death
smrznut frozen
snažan energetic
snijeg snow *n.*
sniježiti snow *v.*
soba room
sok juice
sóko falcon
sol salt
solnjača saltshaker
sos gravy
sova owl
spajanje connection (physical)
sparoga asparagus
spasiti rescue *v.*
spavaća kola sleeping car
spavaona bedroom
spavati sleep
spoznaja consciousness
spojiti bind *v.*
spomenik monument
sposoban capable
sposobnost capability
spremnost willingness
spustiti lower *v.*
sram shame *n.*
sramežljiv shy
sramit se be ashamed
sramota embarrassment
srce heart

srdele sardines
srebro silver
sreća happiness
sredina middle
središte center
srediti arrange; put in order
sresti meet *v.*
sretan happy
srijeda Wednesday
srna doe
srodnost relationship
srpanj July
stablo tree
stajati stand *v.*
staklo (prozorsko) glass (pane of glass)
stalan permanent
stalno constantly
stan apartment
stanovanje habitation
star old
starica old woman
starine antique
starost old age
stav attitude
stegno thigh
stepenište staircase
stići arrive
stid shame *n.*
stipendija scholarship
stiskati press *v.*
sto hundred
stol table
stolica chair

stoljeće century
strah fear
stran (m.) foreign
strana side
stranac foreigner
strani jezik foreign language
strani novac foreign money
strano (nt.) foreign
strašljivac coward
strašno grisly
strast passion
stražar guard *n.*
stric uncle (father's brother)
stroj engine; machine
strop ceiling
strpljivost patience
stručnjak expert
stuba stair
studeni November
student student
stvar thing
stvarno actually; certainly; really
subota Saturday
sûd pan; can
sudac judge *n.*
sudar collision
sudbina destiny
súdio share *n.*
suditi judge *v.*
sudjelovati participate
sudnica court *n.*
suglasan agreeable
suglasit se agree

suh dry *adj.*

sumnjati doubt *v.*

sumrak dusk

sunčane naočale sunglasses

sunčanica sunstroke

sunčanje sunbathe

sunčano sunny

sunce sun

suparnik rival *n.*

suprotan opposite

suprug husband

supruga wife

surov raw

susjed (m.) neighbor

susjeda (f.) neighbor

susjedni neighboring

susjedni adjoining; adjacent

sutra tomorrow

suvlasnik partner

suza tear *n.*

sûziti narrow *v.*

svađati se quarrel *v.*

svadba wedding

svaki each

svaki put every time

sve jedno all the same

svečanost festival

svećenik priest

svekar father-in-law (husband's father)

svekoliko everything

svekrva mother-in-law (husband's mother)

svemir universe

svetac saint

svi all (pl.)
svibanj May
svih all sorts of
svih vrsta all kinds of
svijeća lamp
svjećnjak chandelier
svijet world
svila silk
svitanje daybreak
svjedočiti testify
svjedok witness *n.*
svjest consciousness
svjetlo light *n.*
svjetski worldly
svjež fresh
svojstvo quality; attribute
svrbiti itch *v.*
svršetak end *n.*
svući undress
svugdje everywhere

Š

šah chess
šaka fist
šala joke *n.*
šalica cup
šaran pike (fish)
šareno polka dot
šaš reeds
šator tent

šećer sugar
šešir hat
šest six
šestina one sixth of
šestorica six of them
šesti sixth
šesnaest sixteen
šezdeset sixty
šest sto six hundred
ševa skylark
šibice matches
šišati se haircut
šišmiš bat
širi wider
širina width
širok wide
škola school *n.*
školovanje schooling
školjka shell
Škotska Scotland
škrga gill
škrob starch *n.*
škrt stingy
šljiva plum
šljivovica plum brandy
šljunak gravel
šofer driver
špijun spy *n.*
Španjolska Spain
šport sport
šta what
štala stable
štediti save *v.*

štednjak kitchen range
šteta damage *n.*
štititi protect *v.*
što dalje as far as
što prije as soon as
što vise as many as
šum noise
šuma forest
šupalj hollow
šuštati rustle *v.*
Švicarska Switzerland
Švedska Sweden
Šveđanin Swede

T

ta (f.) that
taj (m.) that
tajno secretly
takmičenje competition
takmičiti se compete
tako so
također also; too
taksa tax *n.*
taksi taxi
Talijan Italian
tama darkness
taman gloomy; dark
tamo there
tanak thin
tanjur plate
taoc hostage

taška handbag
tavanica ceiling
teći flow *v.*
teká notebook
tele calf
telefon telephone *n.*
telefonom by phone
teletina veal
televizor television
temelj foundation
teško difficult
tetka aunt
têžák heavy
težina weight *n.*
ti you (infor.)
tiho quietly; silently
tikva pumpkin
tišina silence
tisuća thousand
tjedan week
tjelo body
tjelovježba gymnastics
tjerati chase *v.*
tjesan tight
tješiti console *v.*
tjesto dough
tkati weave
tko who
tlak pressure
to this; it; that
točan exact; correct
točka period
to sve all

tok flow *v.*
toliko mnogo so many
tonuti sink *v.*
topao warm
toplina temperature
toranj tower
tovar freight
trajati last *v.*
trava grass
travanj April
tražiti seek
trčati run *v.*
trebati need *v.*
treći third
trećina one third
trenerka sweat suit
trenutak moment
tresak crash *n.*
trešnja cherry
trg market; town square
tri three
trideset thirty
trinaest thirteen
trka race *n.*
trolejbus trackless trolley
trošak expense
trošitelj droge drug addict
trošiti droge to use drugs
troškovi expenses
trpjeti suffer
truba trumpet
trud effort
tu here

tucet dozen
tući se fight *v.*
tuča fight *n.*
tuđin foreigner
tuga grief; sorrow
tup dull
turist tourist
Turska Turkey
tuš shower (bath)
tužan sad
tužno sadly
tvoj (m.) your (infor.)
tvoja (f.) your (infor.)
tvoje (nt.) your (infor)
tvornica factory
tvrditi affirm

U

u in
u dvoje double
u međuvremenu meanwhile
u pravu si downright
u stvari indeed
u svakom slučaju in any case
ubiti kill
ubojica murderer
ubojstvo murder *n.*
ubosti stab *v.*
učenica (f.) pupil
učenik (m.) pupil
učenje learning

učestvovanje participation
ući get in; enter
učitelj (m.) teacher
učiteljica (f.) teacher
učiti study *v.*
učtiv polite
udarac hit *n.*
udariti hit *v.*
udata (f.) married
udica hook
udobnost comfort *n.*
udovac widower
udovica widow
udruženi associated
udvarati courting
ugalj coal
ugao corner; angle
ugasiti extinguish
uglačati glaze *v.*
ugovor agreement; contract
ugristi bite *v.*
uho; uši (pl.) ear; ears
uhvatiti catch *v.*
uistinu for sure
ujak uncle (mother's brother)
ujesti sting *v.*
ukrasti steal
ukus taste; style
ukusno tasty
ulaz entry; gate
ulaz se plaća a fee is charged
ulica street
uliti pour

ulje oil
uljepšan decorated
uljepšati decorate *v.*
ulog deposit (money)
umak sauce
umijeće skill; talent
umjesto in place of
umjetnik artist
umjetnost art
umoran tired
umrijeti die *v.*
unajmiti rent *v.*
uništen ruined; destroyed
uništiti destroy; exterminate
univerzitet university
unuk grandson
unuka granddaughter
unutra inside
uostalom after all
upaliti svjetlo switch on lights
upasti u fall into
upisat se register *v.*
uplašit se panic *v.*
uplatiti pay into
uporedivo comparatively
upoznati get to know
upozorenje precaution
upravitelj manager
upravljati control; manage *v.*
uprkos despite
uréd office
urod harvest *n.*
usamljen lonely

usisavač prašine vacuum cleaner
uskoro before long; soon
Uskrs Easter
usluga favor *n.*
uslužan courteous
uspjeh success
usredotočiti concentrate
usta mouth
ustati get up
ustav constitution
uštipak doughnut
ustrajan persistent
ustrajati persist *v.*
usuti pour *v.*
uteći escape; run away
utopiti se drown *v.*
utorak Tuesday
uvjek always
uvjeren convinced
uvjeriti assure *v.*
uvreda insult *n.*
uvrijediti insult *v.*
uzalud in vain
užas horror
užasno grisly; horrible
uzastopno regularly
uzbuđen excited
uzbuna alarm *n.*
uzeti take *v.*
uzetost paralysis; seizure
uzgajati cultivate
uživati rejoice *v.*
uznemiren annoyed; disturbed

uznemirenje disturbance
uzništvo jail *n.*
uzrok cause *n.*
užurbanost activity

V

vadičep corkscrew
vaga scale
vagati weight *v.*
vagon wagon
vam (nt.) you (for.)
vangradski okoliš countryside
vani outside
vas (f.) you (for.)
vaš (m.) your (for.)
vaša (f.) your (for.)
vaše (nt.) your (for.)
vatra fire (small)
vatromet fireworks
vaze crockery
već already
večer evening
večera supper
veći bigger; greater
većina majority
veličina size
velik big; great
veljača February
vena vein
veranda porch

veš underwear
veseliti se cheer v.
veselje festivity
veselo merrily
vi (m.) you (for.)
vidik sight
viditi see v.
vijolina violin
vikati shout v.
viljuška fork
vino wine
više more
visina height
višnja sour cherry
visok high
viza visa
vječnost eternity
vjek age
vjekovima through the ages
vjernost fidelity
vjeroispovjest faith; religion
vjerovati believe v.
vješalica hanger
vjetar wind
vjeverica squirrel
vježba exercise n.
vježbati exercise v.
vlada government
vlak train n.
vlasnik owner
vlasništvo ownership
vlastiti own

vlažan moist
voće fruit
vođa leader
voda water
vodič guide *n.*
voditi lead *v.*
vodopad waterfall
vojska army
vol ox
voliti like *v.*
volja will *n.*
voštana svijeća candle
vozač driver
vozačka dozvola driver's license
vozilo vehicle
voziti drive *v.*
vozna karta ticket
vrabac sparrow
vrat neck
vrata door
vratit se return *v.*
vrč glass (tumbler)
vreća bag
vrenje fermentation
vrijednost value *n.*
vrijeme weather
vrlina virtue
vrlo very
vrlo daleko od far away from
vrt garden
vruć hot
vuk wolf
vuna wool

Z

za after; for
za vrijeme during
zabava party
zabavljat se enjoy oneself
zabavljati entertain
zaboraviti forget *v.*
zabraniti forbid *v.*
zabrinut sa concerned with
začuđen astonished
zadah smell *n.*
zadnji last
zadovoljan satisfied
zadovoljiti please *v.*
zadovoljstvo pleasure
zadušno stuffy
zagonetka mystery
zagrijati warm up
zagrliti embrace *v.*
zahod toilet
zahrđati rust *v.*
zahtjev demand *n.*
zahtjevati demand *v.*
zahvalan thankful
zahvaliti thank *v.*
zainteresiran to be interested in
zajednički mutual
zajedno together
zakasniti to be late
zakleti se swear *v.*
zakletva pledge *n.*
zaključak conclusion

zakon law
zaljubiti se fall in love
zamak castle
zamisao sense; imagination
zamisliti imagine *v.*
zamjena substitute *n.*
zamotati wrap up *v.*
zanemariti neglect *v.*
zanimanje profession
zanimljiv interesting
zao bad; vile
zaokret turn *n.*
zaostati lag behind
zaoštriti sharpen *v.*
zaova sister-in-law (husband's sister)
zapad west
zapadni western
zapaljač lighter
zapaljiv inflammable
zapaljivo combustive
zapamtiti remember *v.*
zapaziti notice *v.*
zaposliti hire *v.*
zaraditi earn *v.*
zarez comma
zaručen engaged
zaručnica (f.) fiancée
zaručnik (m.) fiancé
zasititi saturate *v.*
zasjedanje session
zaslužiti earn *v.*
zasnovano be based on
zastava flag

zašto what for; why
zastupnik representative
zato because
zatvor jail; prison
zatvoren closed
zatvoriti arrest; lock up
zaustaviti stop *v.*
zauzet engaged; occupied
zauzeti occupy; capture
zaviditi envy *v.*
zavist envy *n.*
zavjesa curtain
zavod institute
završetak conclusion
završetak tjedna weekend
zbirka collection
zbogom good-bye; go with God
zbor chorus
zdjela bowl
zdrav healthy
zdravica toast *n.*
zdravlje health
zebra zebra
zec rabbit
zelen green
zemlja land; soil
zemljoposjednik farmer
zemljovid map
zet son-in-law
zgrada building
zid wall
zima winter
ziman wintry

zjevati yawn *v.*
zlatni golden
zlato gold
zlo evil; harm *n.*
zloba malice
zločin crime
zločinac criminal
zmija snake
značenje meaning
značiti mean *v.*
znak sign *n.*
znati know *v.*
znatiželjan curious
znoj perspiration; sweat
zona zone
zoologija zoology
zoološki vrt zoo
zračna pošta airmail
zrak air
zrakoplov airplane
zreo ripe
zrno grain
zub tooth
zubar dentist
zubna proteza denture
zvati call *v.*
zvati telefonom call up by phone

Ž

žaba frog
žagor murmur *n.*

žaliti mourn *v.*
žalost sorrow
žalostan sorry
žao mi je I am sorry
žaoka sting *n.*
žar warmth; glow
žarulja lightbulb
žeđ thirst
žedan (m.) thirsty
žedna (f.) thirsty
želja wish
željezo steel
željeznica railroad
želiti wish *v.*
želudac stomach
žena wife; woman
ženka female (all species)
žensko female (human)
ženski feminine
ženidba wedding
žica wire
Židov Jew
Židovski Jewish
žig stamp *n.*
žila vein
žlica spoon
žir acorn
živ alive
živá mercury
živac nerve
živiti live *v.*
život life
životinja animal

životopis biography
žlijezda gland
žuč bile
žumance yolk
žulj blister *n.*
župa parish
žut yellow
žurba haste
žuriti se hurry *v.*
žvakaća guma chewing gum
žvakati chew *v.*

ENGLISH-CROATIAN DICTIONARY

A

able mogu
about oko; u
above nad
above all iznad svega
accident nesretan slučaj; nesreća
accountant knjigovođa
accumulate nagomilati
accuse okriviti
accustomed naviknut
acknowledge priznati
acquaintance poznanik
act n. čin; odluka
action djelovanje
activity djelatnost; užurbanost
actor glumac
actress glumica
actual sadašnji; stvarni
actually stvarno
additional dodatni
address n. adresa
adjoining susjedni; blizak
admire diviti se
adult odrasla osoba; punoljetan
adventure pustolovina; smjelost
advertisement oglas
advice savjet
advise savjetovati
affirm tvrditi

Africa Afrika
after po; za; iza
after all uostalom; premda
afternoon popodne
again iznova; još jednom
against protiv
age starost; vjek
agree pristati; suglasit se
agreeable suglasan
agreement ugovor; pristanak
air zrak
airmail zračna pošta
airplane zrakoplov
airport aerodrom
alarm uzbuna
alas jao; ajme
alcohol alkohol
alcoholic alkoholičar
all to sve
all (pl.) svi
all at once odjednom
all kinds of svih vrsta
all sorts of raznih vrsta
all the same sve jedno
allow dozvoliti
almost za malo
alone sam (m.); sama (f.); samo (nt.)
already već
also također
although iako; premda
always uvjek
ambitious častoljubiv

ambulance ambulanta
America Amerika
American Američki
American man Amerikanac
American woman Amerikanka
and a; i
anger n. ljutnja; gnjev
angry ljutit
animal životinja
anniversary godišnjica
announce proglasiti
annoying dosadan
another jedan drugi
anthem himna
antique starine
anyone bilo tko
anytime bilo kad
apartment stân
appear pojavit se
apple jabuka
appropriate pogodan; podesan
apricot kajsija
April travanj
arm ruka
armchair fotelja
army vojska
around okolo
arranged pripremljeno
arrest v. zatvoriti
arrival dolazak
arrive stići; doputovati
arrive by air doći zrakoplovom

arrive on time doći na vrijeme
art umjetnost
artery žila kucavica; arterija
article članak
artist umjetnik
as far as što dalje
ashamed (to be) sramit se
ashtray pepeljara
Asia Azija
ask v. pitati
as many as što više
asparagus sparoga
assemble v. skupit se
associated udruženi
as soon as što prije
assure uvjeriti; ubjediti
astonished začuđen
at kod; pri
at all ikako
at least napokon
at once odmah; sád
at other times drugom prilikom
attack napad
attractive privlačan (m.); privlačna (f.)
at your place kod tvoje kuće
audience slušaoci
August kolovoz
aunt tetka
Austria Austrija
autumn jesen
average prosječan
away dalje

B

baby djete
bachelor neženja
back leđa
backside poleđina
bacon slanina
bad zao
bad habit loša navika
bag vreća
bake v. peći
baker pekar
balcony balkon
bald ćelav
ball lopta
ball (gala) ples
ballet balet
banana banana
band (orchestra) orkestar
bank banka
barely ječam
bark n. kora
bark v. lajati
barrel bačva
basketball košarka
bathtub kâda
bathe v. kupati se
bathroom kupaona
battle n. boj
be v. biti
be awake biti budan
be based on zasnovano na
be born rodit se
be it (so be it) néká; néká bude

be late zakasniti
be of use biti potreban
be quiet šutiti
be right bit u pravu
be sad biti tužan
beach plaža
bean grah
bear medvjed
bearded bradat
beauty ljepota
because jer; zato
become postati
become evident biti očevidno
become extinct izumrijeti
become insane poluditi
become sober otrijeznit se
bed postelja; krevet
bedroom spavaona
bee pčela
beef govedina
beer pivo
beet cikla
before long uskoro
beggar prosjak
begin početi
beginning početak
behind iza
belch v. podrignuti
believe vjerovati
belt remen; pâs
bench klupa
berry jagoda
besides osim
besides that osim toga

best najbolji
better bolji
between između
bicycle bicikl
big velik
bind v. spojiti
biography životopis
biology biologija
bird ptica
birthday rođendan
bite v. ugristi
bitter gorak
black crn
blanket pokrivač; deka
bless v. blagosloviti
bliss blaženstvo
blister n. žulj
blood krv
blouse bluza
blue plav
boat brod
body tjelo
bone kost
book knjiga
bookkeeping knjigovodstvo
border granica
boring dosadan
boss nadzornik; šef
both obadva
bottle flaša
bottom dno
bowl zdjela

box kutija
boy dječak
brain mozak
brake n. kočnica
branch grana
brandy rakija
brave hrabar
bread kruh
break v. slomiti
breakfast doručak
breast dojka; grudi
breathe v. disati
breeze lahor
bride mlâdâ
bridegroom mladoženja
bridge môst
brief kratkotrajan
bring donijeti
broadcast n. razglas
broaden proširiti
bronze bronza
broth juha
brother brát
brother-in-law djever (husband's brother)
brother-in-law šurjak (wife's brother)
brown smeđ
bruise n. modrica
brush n. četka
buffet bufet
bug insekt
build graditi
builder graditelj
building n. zgrada

building (under construction) građevina
bull bik
bulletin board oglasna ploča
bun žemička
burn v. goriti
bury v. pokopati
bus autobus
bus stop autobusna stanica
bush grm
business posao
bustle metež; žurba
busy poslovan
but but; nego
butter maslo
butterfly leptir
button dugme
buy v. kupiti

C

cabbage kupus
caffeine kofein
cake kolač
calf tele
call v. zvati
call up by phone zvati telefonom
called (be) biti pozvan
calm miran
calm down smiri se
camera fotoaparat
can n. konzerva; sud
can v. moći

Canada Kanada
cancel v. poništiti
cancer rak (rana)
candle voštana svijeća
candy bonboni
capability sposobnost
capable sposoban
car samovoz; auto
card karta
care for starat se
caress v. milovati
carp šaran
carrot mrkva
carry v. nositi
carry (by vehicle) dopremit
case n. slučaj
case (in any) u svakom slučaju
cashier blagajnik
castle zamak
cat mačka
catch v. uhvatiti
catch a cold prehladit se
Catholic Katolik
cauliflower cvjetača
cause (responsible for) n. uzrok
caution oprez
cave pećina
ceiling tavanica; strop
celebrate slaviti
celery celer
cellar podrum
cemetery groblje
center središte; centar

central station glavni kolodvor
century stoljeće
ceramic keramika
certainly stvarno
certificate potvrda
chair stolica
chalk kreda
chance n. prilika
chandelier svijećnjak
change n. razmjena
change v. razmjeniti
character osobina; karakter
charm n. ljepota
charm v. opčarati; zanijeti
chase v. tjerati
cheap jeftin
check n. ček; priznanica
check v. kontrolirati; spriječiti
cheek obraz
cheer v. veseliti se; klicati
cheese sir
cherry trešnja
chess šah
chest grudi
chestnut kesten
chew v. žvakati
chewing gum žvakaća guma
chicken pile
child djete
children djeca
Chinese Kinez
chocolate čokolada
choice izbor

choose v. izabrati
chorus zbor; pjevački
Christmas Božić
Christmas Eve Badnja večer
church crkva
cider kvasina; ocat
cigarette cigareta
cinema kino
cinnamon cimet
circle krug
circus cirkus
citizen građanin
citizen ID osobne isprave
class razred
clean n. čist
clean v. čistiti
clean (house) čistit (kuću)
cleaning čišćenje
cleanliness čistoća
clear jasan
clerk činovnik
climb penjati se
clock sat; zidni
close v. zatvoriti
closed zatvoren
clothing odjeća
cloud oblak
cloudy oblačno
clown komedijaš
club štap; klub
coal ugalj
coast obala
coat kaput

coatroom garderoba

cocoa kakao

cod (fish) bakalar

coffee kava

coffin ljes

coin kovani novac

cold hladno

collar okovratnik

colleague prijatelj (m.); prijateljica (f.)

collection zbirka

collector sabirač

collision sudar

color n. boja

color v. bojati

colored obojan

comb n. česalj

comb v. češljati

combustive zapaljivo

come v. doći

comfort n. udobnost; utjeha

comfort v. tješiti

comma zarez

command n. naredba

commit v. obavezati se

committee odbor

comparatively uporedivo

compassion milost; saćut

compensation nadoknada

compete v. takmičiti se

competition takmičenje

complaint prigovor

complete v. dovršiti

completely sasvim
complexion izgled lica
compliment pohvala
composer skladatelj
computer komputer
computer science nauka o komputeru
concentrate v. usredotočiti; koncentrirati
concerned with zabrinut sa
concert koncert
conclusion odluka; završetak
condition stanje; stav
condolence saučešće
confess v. ispovjediti se
confidence povjerenje
confirmation dokaz; potvrda
congratulate čestitati
congratulations čestitke
congress parlamenat
connection (physical) spajanje
connection (related) srodnost
consciousness svjest; spoznaja
consequence posljedica
console v. tješiti
constantly stalno
constitution ustav
constructed sagrađen
consume v. potrošiti
consumption potrošnja
contemporary savremenik
contract ugovor
control v. upravljati
conversation razgovor

converse v. razgovarati
convict n. osuđenik
convinced uvjeren
cook n. kuhar
cook v. kuhati
cookies keksi
cooking kuhanje
cool adj. hladno
cool v. ohladiti
cooperate sudjelovati
cork čep (od plutva)
corkscrew vadičep
corn kukuruz
corner kut; ugao
correct n. ispravan
correction ispravka
corridor hodnik
cosmos svemir
couch fotelja
cough n. kašalj
could moći
count v. brojiti
country država
countryside vangradski okoliš
couple dvojica
courage odvažnost; kuraž
court sudnica
courteous uslužan
cousin rođak
cover n. pokrivač
cover v. pokriti
coward strašljivac

crab rak

craftsman obrtnik

crash n. tresak; lom

crawl v. puzati

crayfish rječni rak

crazy lud

cream skorup; krema

credit kredit; povjerenje

criminal zločinac

criminal act zločin

crockery vaze; posuđe od gline

cross v. preći preko

crossing raskrsnica

crown kruna

crude oil nepročišćena nafta

crunchy krckavo

cry v. plakati

cucumber krastavac

cultivate v. uzgajati; obrađivati

cup šalica

cure v. izliječiti

cure n. liječenje

curious znatiželjan; radoznao

currants ribizl

currency novac

curtain zavjesa

cushion jastuk

custom običaj

customer mušterija; kupac

customs carina

cut v. prerezati

Czech Čeh

Czech Republic Česka republika

D

dance v. plesati
dance n. ples
daring smjelost
dark taman
darkness tama; mrak
date n. datum
daughter kćer
daughter-in-law nevjesta
day after tomorrow prekosutra
day before yesterday prekjuče
day (good day) dan (dobar dan)
daybreak svitanje
dead mrtav
deaf gluh
dear dragi (m.); draga (f.)
death smrt
debt dûg
deceased pokojni
deceive v. prevariti
December prosinac
deception prevara
decide odlučiti
decorate uljepšati; dekorirati
decorated uljepšan
deep dubok
defend braniti
deformed nakazan
delicate profinjen; delikatan
demand v. zahtjevati
demolish v. razrušiti
dense gust

dentist zubar; dentist
denture zubna proteza
depart odputovati
department odjeljenje
department store robna kuća
depend ovisiti
deposit n. ulog; naslaga
deposit v. uložiti
describe opisati
designation imenovanje
desperate beznadan
despite uprkos
destiny sudbina
destroy uništiti
development razvoj
devoted to odan; privržen
devour proždrijeti
diarrhea proljev
dictionary rječnik
die v. umrijeti
difference razlika
difficult teško
difficulty poteškoća
digest v. probaviti
diligent marljiv
dining blagovanje
dining room blagovaona
direction smjer
director načelnik
dirt smeće; nečistoća
disappear nestati
disappointment razočaranje

disconnect isključiti
discover pronaći; izumiti
disease bolest
disgust n. odvratnost; gađenje
disgusting odvratno
disheveled razbarušen
dishonest nepošten
dislike n. nedopadanje
disobedience neposlušnost
displayed izložen
dissolve rastopiti
distance n. razdaljina
district okrug
disturbance uznemirenje
diverse raznovrstan
divide v. razdjeliti
divorce razvod braka; rastava
do raditi
do (to finish) uraditi; odraditi
doctor liječnik; doktor
doctorate doktorat
doe srna; košuta
dog pás
doll lutka
dollar dolar
donkey magarac
door vrata
dormitory đački dom
double u dvoje; par
doubt v. sumnjati
dough tjesto
doughnut uštipak

do well radi dobro

down (below) doli; ispod

downright u pravu si

dozen tucet; dúzina

draft propuh

dream of sanjati o

dream n. san

dress haljina

dressed (to get) obući se

dressed obučen (m.); obučena (f.)

dried osušen

drink n. piće

drink v. piti

drink up ispiti

drive v. voziti

driver vozač; šofer

driver's license vozačka dozvola

drop n. kap

drown utopiti se

drug droga

drug addict trošitelj droge

drugstore ljekarna; apoteka

drum n. bubanj

drunk pijan

dry suh

duck n. patka

dull tup

dumpling knedla

during za vrijeme

dusk sumrak

dust prašina

duty dužnost

E

each svaki
eagle orao
ear uho; uši (pl.)
early rano
earn zaslužiti; zaraditi
east istok
Easter Uskrs
eastern istočni
easy lako
eat jesti
edge rub; oštrica
education naobrazba
effort napor; trud
egg jaje
egoist sebičan
eight osam
eighteen osamnaest
eighty osamdeset
either billo koji (m.); koja (f.)
either/or ili/ili
elbow lakat
elect v. izabrati
election izbori
electricity električna struja
electronic elektronika
elephant slon
elevator lift; dizalo
eleven jedanaest
eleventh jedanaesti
elsewhere negdje drugdje
embarrassment sramota

embrace v. zagrliti
emergency exit hitni izlaz; izlaz u nuždi
emigration emigracija; izseljenje
empty adj. prazan
encircle v. okružiti
end n. kraj; svršetak
end v. dovršiti; okončati
endure izdržati
enemy neprijatelj
energetic snažan; energičan
engaged zaručen; zauzet
engine stroj
engineer inžinjer
England Engleska
English (in) na engleskom
English (language) Engleski
Englishman Englez
Englishwoman Engleskinja
enjoy oneself zabavljat se
enlist prijavit se
enough dosta
enough time dosta vremena
enrage razdražiti
ensure osigurati
entertain zabavljati
enthusiastic oduševljen
entrance prolaz
entry ulaz
envelope omotnica
envy n. zloba; zavist
envy v. zaviditi
equally jednako
eraser guma za brisanje

escape v. pobjeći; uteći
escape n. bjeg
especially posebno
esteemed cjenjeni
eternity vječnost
Europe Europa
even (in the end) napokon
evening večer
everything svekoliko
every time svaki put
everywhere svugdje
evidently očevidno
examination ispit
example (for) na primjer
example uzorak; primjer
excellent izvrstan
exception iznimka; izuzetak
exceptional izuzetan
exchange n. razmjena
exchange v. razmjeniti
excited uzbuđen
excursion izlet
excuse v. oprostiti
excuse me oprostite mi
exercise v. vježbati
exercise n. vježba
exhausted premoren
exile n. izgnanstvo
exit izlaz
expect očekivati
expense trošak
expenses troškovi
expensive skupo

experience iskustvo
expert poznavaoc; ekspert
explain obrazložiti
express train brzi vlak
extensive rasprostranjen
extent opseg; prostranstvo
exterminate uništiti
extinguish ugasiti
extreme krajnji; ekstremni
eye oko; oči (pl.)
eyebrow obrva
eyeglasses naočale

F

face lice
face-to-face licem u lice
factory tvornica
failure neuspjeh
faint v. pasti u nesvjest
faith vjeroispovjest
falcon soko
fall n. jesen
fall v. pasti
fall down pasti doli
fall ill oboliti
fall in love zaljubiti se
fall into upasti u
fall out ispasti
false lažan
family obitelj
famous slavan

fantastic čudan
far daleko
far away vrlo daleko
farmer zemljoposjednik
fashion običaj; moda
fat debeo (m.); debela (f.); debelo (nt.)
father otac
father's očev
father-in-law (husband's father) svekar
father-in-law (wife's father) punac
fault mâná
favor úslúgá
favorite povlašćen
fear strah
feast gozba
February veljača
fee charged ulaz se plaća
feel v. osjećati
feeling osjećaj
fellow poznanik
female (human) žensko
female (animal) ženka
feminine ženski
fence ograda
fermentation vrenje; fermentacija
fester brže
festival svečanost
festivity veselje
fever groznica
fiancé zaručnik (m.)
fiancée zaručnica (f.)
fidelity vjernost
field polje

fifteen petnaest
fifth peti
fiftieth pedeseti
fifty pedeset
fight n. boj; tuča
figure oblik
filling plomba
fill up napuni; nalij
finally konačno; napokon
financial novčani
find v. naći
finger prst
finish v. dovršiti
fire (small) vatra
fire (big) požar
fireworks vatromet
firm čvrst; odlučan
first (number one) prvi
first floor prizemlje
fish n. riba
five pet
fix (to prepare) pripraviti
fix (to repair) popraviti
flag zastava
flatter v. hvalisati
flaw mana; kvar
flexible gibak
floor pod
floor (story) kat
flour brašno
flow n. tok
flow v. teći
flower cvijet

flu gripa
fly v. letiti
fly n. muha
fog magla
follow slijediti
food jelo
fool n. budala
foot n. stopalo
foot (on) pješke; nanoge
for za
forbid zabraniti
force (by) sila; na silu
forecast n. prognoza
forecast v. prognozirati
forehead čelo
foreign strano; nepoznato
foreign language strani jezik
foreign money strani novac
foreigner tuđin; stranac
forenoon (late morning) prije podne
forest šuma
forget zaboraviti
forgive oprostiti
fork viljuška
for sure stvarno; uistinu
fortunately sa srećom
forward naprijed
foundation temelj
four četiri (m.); četiri (f.); četvero (nt.)
fourteen četrnaest
fracture pukotina
fragile krhki
France Francuska

free (physically) slobodan
freedom sloboda
freethinking slobodouman
freight tovar
Frenchman Francuz
Frenchwoman Francuskinja
fresh svjež
Friday petak
fried prženi
friend (close) prijatelj (m.); prijateljica (f.)
frivolous lakouman
frog žaba
from od
from above odozgor
from an early age od rane mladosti
from below odozdol
from here odavde
from inside iznutra
from when odkad
from where odakle
front (in) sprijeda
front of (in) ispred
frost mraz
frozen smrznut
fruit voće
fry v. popržiti
fuel gorivo
full pun
funnel n. ljevak
funny smješan
fur coat krzneni kaput
furious ljutit
furniture namještaj

further dalje
future budućnost

G

gall bladder žuč
game igra
garage garaža
garbage dump smetište
garden vrt
garlic češnjak
gasoline benzin
gate ulaz; prolaz
gather sakupljati
gathering skup; mnoštvo
generally općenito
generosity darežljivost
German Njemac
German woman Njemica
Germany Njemačka
get dobit; dohvatit
get drunk opit se
get in ući
get out izići
get to know upoznati
get up ustati
get wet pokisnuti
gift dar
gin džin
girl djevojka
give dati
give birth roditi

gland žlijezda
glass (tumbler) pehar; vrč
glass (pane of) staklo (prozorsko)
glaze uglačati
globe globus
gloomy mračan; taman
glove rukavica
glue n. ljepilo
glue v. lijepiti
go ići
go ahead samo produži
go out ići u grad
go with God zbogom
goal cilj; namjera
God Bog
gold zlato
golden zlatni; pozlaćen
good dobro
good-bye do viđenja
good night laku noć
goods roba široke potrošnje
goose guska
gossip ogovaranje
government vlada
grain zrno
granddad djed
granddaughter unuka
grandmother baba; baka
grandson unuk
grape grožđe
grass trava
grave grob
gravy sos; umak

gray sjed
grease mast
great važan; velik
greater veći
green zelen
greeting pozdrav
grief tuga; žalost
grind up samljeti
grisly strašno; užasno
grits griz
group skupina
grow bald oćelaviti
grow up odrasti
guarantee n. garancija; osiguranje
guarantee v. osigurati
guest gost
guide vodič
guitar gitara
gymnastics tjelovježba
gypsy Ciganin

H

habit navika; običaj
habitation stan; stanovanje
hair kosa
hairdo frizura
hairdresser frizer (m.); frizerka (f.)
hairy dlakav
half pola
half a kilo pola kila
hall dvorana

ham pršut; šunka
hand ruka
handbag taška
handkerchief rupčić; maramica
hang objesiti
hanger vješalica
happiness sreća
happy sretan
hardly jedva; s mukom
harm zlo; povreda
harvest n. urod; žetva
harvest v. žeti
hat šešir
hate n. mržnja
hate v. mrziti
have imati
he on
head glava
head waiter nadkonobar
health zdravlje
healthy zdrav
hear čuti
heart srce
heaven nebo
heavy têžak
height visina
hell pakao
hello halo
help n. pomoć
help v. pomoći
help yourself pomozi se
her nju
here tu; ovdje

hi zdravo
hidden sakrit
high visok
hill brdo; brijeg
hillside proplanak
him on
hire zaposliti
his njegov
historical povjesni
history povijest
hit n. udarac
hit v. udariti
hit (target) pogoditi metu
hockey hokej
hold v. držati
hole rupa
holiday praznik
home kuća
home (at) kod kuće
honey med
honeymoon medeni mjesec
honor n. čast
hook kuka; udica
hope n. nada
hope v. nadati se
horror užas
horse konj
hospital bolnica
hostage taoc
hot vruć
hotel hotel
hour jedan sat

house kuća
household domaćinstvo
housewife kućanica
how kako
however bilo tko
how many koliko
huge ogroman
human ljudski
hundred sto
Hungarian Mađar
hunger n. glad
hungry gladan
hunter lovac
hurricane orkan
hurry n. požuri
hurry v. žuriti
husband suprug; muž

I

ice lêd
ice cream sladoled
idea ideja
identity card osobna karta
if ako
illegitimate nezakonit
illness bólêst
imagine zamisliti
immoral nemoralan; razvratan
immortal bezsmrtan
impatient nestrpljiv

impression dojam
improper nepravilan
improve poboljšati
in u
indeed stvarno; u stvari
independent samostalan; neovisan
industry radinost; industrija
inflammable zapaljiv
information obavještenje
ingratitude nezahvalnost
inherit naslijediti
inheritance nasljedstvo
injured ozlijeđen
injury ozljeda
inquire pitati
insane lud; umobolan
insect kukac
inside iznutra
insult n. uvreda
insult v. uvrijediti
insurance osiguranje
interested in (be) zainteresiran
interesting zanimljiv
intermission pauza
international međunarodni
interpreter prevodilac
interrogation istraga
intestines crijeva
investigate istraživati
invite v. pozvati
iron (metal) željezo; gvožđe

iron n. pegla
iron v. peglati
irregular neredovit
irresponsible neodgovoran
irritate izazivati
island otok
Italian Talijan
Italy Italija
itch v. svrbiti
its njegov

J

jacket kaput
jail n. uzništvo; zatvor
jam mermelada
January sječanj
Japanese Japanac (m.); Japanka (f.)
jealousy ljubomora
Jew Židov
jewel nakit
Jewish židovski
joke n. šala
joke v. šalit se
judge n. sudac
judge v. suditi
juice sok
July srpanj
jump n. skok
jump v. skočiti
June lipanj
justice Pravda

K

kerchief marama
key ključ
kidney bubreg
kill v. ubiti
kilogram kilo
kindness dobrota
kiss n. poljubac
kiss v. poljubiti
kissing ljubljenje
kitchen kuhinja
knee koljeno
knife nož
knit v. plesti
knock v. kucati
know znati
knowledge znanje

L

lacking nedostaje
lad mladić
lag behind zaostati
lake jezero
lamb janja
lamp svijeća
land kopno; zemlja
language (speech) jezik
lard mast
last adj. zadnji; posljednji
last v. trajati

last will oporuka
last year lani
late adj. kasno
late (to be) v. zakasniti
later kasnije
laugh at ismijavati
law zakon
lawyer pravnik
laying down ležati
lazy lijen
lead v. voditi
leader vođa
learning učenje
leave napustiti
left lijevi
leftovers ostatci
leg noga
lemon limun
lend posudit
length dužina
lentil leća
less manje
lesson lekcija
let dozvoliti
letter pismo
liberation oslobođenje
library knjižnica
lie down leći na
life život
lift v. podignut
light adj. lako
light n. svjetlo
light v. osvjetlit

lightbulb žarulja
lightning sjevanje
lighter zapaljač
like v. voliti
like this ovako
line linija
lion lav
lipstick ruž
literature književnost
little malo
live živjeti
livelihood opstanak
liver jetra
living življenje
living room dnevna soba
local mjesni
locate pronaći
lock up zatvoriti
lonely usamljen
long dugo
long ago davno
look n. pogled
look v. gledati
look after brinuti se
lose izgubiti
lost izgublejen
loud glasan
love n. ljubav
love v. voliti
lover ljubavnik
low nisko
lower adj. donji
lower v. spustiti

lunch ručak
lungs pluća
luxury obilje

M

machine stroj
mad lud
madman luđak
magazine časopis
magnify povećati
main glavni
maintain održavati
majority većina
make napraviti
make a mistake pogriješiti
make easier olakšati
make possible omogućiti
make smaller smanjiti
make up v. nadoknaditi
make wide razširiti
man čovjek
manager upravitelj
manual ručni
many mnogo
map zemljovid; karta
March ožujak
market trg
married oženjen (m.); udata (f.)
mass (religious service) misa
match n. šibice
material materijal
mathematics matematika

mattress madrac
May svibanj
maybe možda
me ja; meni; mi
meal jelo
mean v. značiti
meaning značenje
meanwhile u međutim
measure v. mjeriti
measure n. mjera
meat meso
medicine lijek; medicina
meet v. sresti
meeting sastanak
melon melon
member član
memory pamćenje
mercy milost
merrily veselo
meter metar
middle sredina
midnight ponoć
midwife babica
milk mlijeko
mind n. razum
mine moj (m.); moja (f.); moje (nt.)
mineral kristal; mineral
minor maloljetan
minute minuta
mirror ogledalo
miser škrtac
miserable jadan
Miss gospođica

Mrs. gospođa
Mr. gospodin
mistake n. greška
mistrust nepovjerenje
misunderstand ne razumjeti
misunderstanding nesporazum
mix smješati
modern suvremen; moderan
modesty skromnost
moist vlažan
moldy pljesnivo
moment trenutak
Monday ponedjeljak
money novac
money (coins) kovani novac
monk fratar
monkey majmun
month mjesec (dana)
monument spomenik
mood raspoloženje
moon mjesec
moral vrlina; moral
more više
morning jutro
mosquito komarac
most najviše
mostly najčešće
mother majka; mama
mother's majčin
mother-in-law (husband's mother) svekrva
mother-in-law (wife's mother) punica
motion gibanje
motorcycle motorcikl

mountain gora
mouse miš
mouth usta
move n. potez
move v. preseliti
move out izseliti se
movie kino
much mnogo
mud blato
mug šalica
multiplication množenje
murder ubojstvo
murderer ubojica
muscle mišica
museum muzej
mushroom gljiva
music glazba; muzika
must v. morati
mustache brkovi
mute nijem
mutual zajednički
mystery zagonetka

N

naive bezazlen
naked go
name ime
name's day imendan
napkin salveta
narrow n. uzak
narrow v. sûziti

nation nacija; narod
national narodni
national costume narodna nošnja
native n. domorodac
nature priroda
navel pupak
near blizu; pri; do
near by nedaleko
necessary potrebno
necessity potreba
neck vrat
necktie kravata
need n. potreba
need v. trebati
needle igla
negative negativan
neglect n. nemar
neglect v. zanemariti
neighbor susjed (m.); susjeda (f.)
neighboring susjedni
neither/nor ni/niti
nephew sinovac (brother's son); sestric (sister's son)
nerve živac
never nikad
new novi
New Year's Eve Silvestrovo
news novost
newspaper novine
next idući; sljedeći
next to do njega
next to each other jedan do drugog
nice prijatan
nickname nadimak

niece nećakinja
night noć
nine devet
nineteen devetnaest
nineteenth devetnaesti
ninety devedeset
ninth deveti
no ne
nobody nitko
no doubt bez dvojbe
noisy bučan
none nijedan (m.); nijedna (f.); nijedn (nt.)
nonsense besmislica
noodles rezanci
normal normalan; pravilan
north sjever
northern sjeverni
nose nos
note nota
notebook têká; bilježnica
not far nedaleko
nothing ništa
notice n. oglas
notice v. zapaziti
not only ne samo
nourishment hranjivost
novel novela
November studeni
now sád
nowhere nigdje
number broj
nun časna sestra

nurse bolničarka
nut orah

O

oak hrast; dub
obedient poslušan
object n. predmet; stvar
object v. prigovarati
obtain nabaviti
occupied zauzet
occurrence događaj
ocean ocean
October listopad
of course pá dá; naravno
offer n. ponuda
offer v. ponuditi
office uréd
often često
oil ulje
old star
old age starost
old woman starica
on na
once jednom
one jedan (m.); jedna (f.); jedno (nt.)
one may može se
oneself sam; sebe
one third trećina
onion lúk
only jedino
on time na vrijeme

open n. otvoreno
open v. otvoriti
opener otvarač
opinion mišljenje
opportunity prilika
opposite suprotan
orange adj. narančast (m.); narančasta (f.)
orange n. naranča
order n. mir
order v. naručiti
order (place an) narudžba
ordinary običan
organization organizacija
organize srediti; organizirati
orphan sirota
other neki drugi
otherwise inače
our naš (n.); naša (f.); naše (nt.)
outpatient department ambulanta
outside vani
owl sova
own vlastiti
owner vlasnik
ownership vlasništvo
ox vol
oyster ostriga

P

package omotak; paket
pain bolovi
painting n. slika

painting v. bojati
pair par
pale blijed
palm dlan
panic v. uplašit se
paper papir
paprika paprika
paradise raj
paralysis uzetost
parent roditelj
parish župa
park park
parsley petrusim
part n. dio
participation učestvovanje
partner suvlasnik
party zabava
pass v. proći
passage prolaz
passenger train putnički vlak
passport putna isprava; pasport
past prošlost
pastry pecivo
patience strpljivost
patient strpljiv; bolesnik; pacijent
patrol n. izvidnica; patrola
pay n. plaća
pay v. platiti
pay extra doplatiti
pay into uplatiti
pay out isplatiti
peace mir
peach breskva

pear kruška
peas biži
peasant seljak
penalty globa
pencil olovka
penguin pingvin
pension mirovina
people narod
perfect savršen
perform izvesti
perfume miris; parfem
perhaps možda
perish nestati
permanent stalan
permission dozvola
persist ustrajati
persistent ustrajan
person osoba
perspiration znoj
pest štetočina
petroleum nafta
pharmacy ljekarna
philosophy filozofija
phone (by) telefonom
photograph fotografija
physics fizika
piano klavir
pick brati
picture n. slika
piece komad
pig prase; svinja
pike (fish) štuka
pillow jastuk

pillowcase jastučna navlaka
pilot pilot; kormilar
pineapple ananas
pine tree bor
pink ružičast
pipe lula
pit jama
place n. mjesto
place v. postaviti
plain jednostavan
plan n. plan
planning planiranje
plant n. biljka
plant v. posaditi
planted posađeno
plate tanjur
play n. igra
play v. igrati se
player igrač
please molim
please v. zadovoljiti
pleasure zadovoljstvo
pledge n. zakletva
plentiful obilan
plug čep
plum šljiva
plum brandy šljivovica
pocket džep
poem pjesma
poison otrov
poisonous otrovan
Poland Poljska
policeman oružnik

police station oružnička postaja
polite učtiv
poor siromah
popcorn pucki
poppy seed mak
poppy seed cake mahovnjača
popular poznat
porch veranda
pork prasetina
porter nosač
portion porcija
possession imetak; vlasništvo
possibility mogućnost
postcard razglednica
post office pošta
potato krompir
poultry perad
pour uliti; usuti
poverty siromaštvo
power môć
praise n. hvala
praise v. hvaliti
pray v. moliti se
precaution upozorenje
precise precizno
pregnant noseća
prehistoric predpovjesni
prepare pripremiti; pripraviti
present n. sadašnjost; prisutan
present v. darovati
press n. novinarstvo
press v. stiskati

pressure tlak
pretty lijepa
price n. cjena
pride ponos; oholost
priest svećenik
prison zatvor
private osobni
probably moguće
processed prerađeno
produce n. proizvod
produce v. proizvesti
production proizvodnja
profession zanimanje
professor profesor
profitable rentabilan
program program
promise obećanje
proof dokaz
proper ispravan
protect braniti
protection obrana
proud ohol
prove dokazati
proverb poslovica
public društveni
pudding puding
pull povući
pull out izvući
pulse puls; bilo
pumpkin tikva
punishment kazna
pupil učenik
purchase kupnja

purple purpuran
put down položiti

Q

quality vrijednost
quarrel n. svađa
quarrel v. svađati se
quarter četvrt
question pitanje
quick brz
quickly brzo
quiet n. tih
quiet v. šutjeti

R

rabbit zec
race n. trka
race v. utrkivat se
radio radio
radish rotkvica
railroad car željeznička kola
rain n. kiša
rain v. kišiti
raise podići
ram ovan
rape n. silovanje
rape v. silovati
rare izniman
raspberry drink malinovac

rat štakor
rather radije
raw sirov; surov
read v. čitati
reading čitanje
ready adj. pripreman
really stvarno
reason razum; razlog; povod
recall opozvati
receipt potvrda
recognize prepoznati
recommend preporučiti
record (disk) gramofonska ploča
record player gramofon
recovery ozdravljenje
red crven
refresh osvježiti
refreshment osvježujuće piće
refugee izbjeglica
region oblast
register upisat se
regularly uzastopno
relationship srodnost
relative rođak
relief olakšanje
religion vjeroispovjest
reluctant neodlučan
remain ostati
remember zapamtiti
rent v. iznajmiti
rent n. najamnina; stanarina
repeat v. ponoviti
report n. prijava

report v. izvjestiti; prijaviti se

representative zastupnik

request n. zahtjev

rescue v. spasiti

research n. naučno istraživanje

research v. istraživati

residence obitavalište

respect n. poštivanje

respect v. poštivati

respectable poštovan

responsibility odgovornost

rest n. počinak

rest v. počivati

restaurant gostiona

restructuring preobradba

return v. vratit (se)

reveal ispoljiti; otkriti

revenge osveta

reverse promjenit smjer

rheumatism reuma

rib rebro

rice riža

rich bogat

ride v. jašiti

riding jašenje

right pravo

right on tačno na

ring n. prsten

ring v. zvoniti

rip v. rasparati

ripe zreo

rival suparnik

river rjeka

road put; cesta
roast n. pečenje
roast v. peći
roast beef pečena govedina
roasted pečen
robber lopov; tat
robot robot
roof krov
room soba
rooster pjetao
rose ruža
rotten gnjili
round okrugao
route n. pravac; put
rug karpet; tepih
ruined uništen
run v. trčati
run away uteći
run off v. odteći
Russian Rus (m.); Ruskinja (f.)
rust n. hrđa
rust v. zahrđati

S

sad tužan; žalostan
sadly tužno
safety sigurnost
sail n. jedro
sail v. jedriti
saint svetac
salad salata

salami salama
salary plata
sale prodaja
salesman prodavač
saleswoman prodavačica
salmon losos
salt sol
saltshaker solnjača
salty slan
sandwich sendvić
sardines srdele
satisfied zadovoljan
saturate zasititi
Saturday subota
sauce umak
saucepan kotlić; lonac
sausage kobasica
save v. štediti
say v. reći
scale vaga
scarf šal
schedule raspored
scholarship stipendija
school škola
science nauka
scientist naučenjak
scissors nožice
sea more
search potražnja
season godišnje doba
second adj. drugi
second n. sekunda

secretly tajno

see viditi

seek tražiti

seem v. činiti se; izgledati

seizure zapljena; otmica

seldom rijetko

self sam; sebi; si

self-confidence samo uvjerenje

self-service samoposluga

sell prodati

send poslati

sense čulo; smisao

sensitive osjetljiv

sentence v. osuditi

sentence (grammar) rečenica

separation rastava; razvod

September rujan

serious ozbiljan

serve služiti

service služba

session zasjedanje

seven sedam

seventeen sedamnaest

seventy sedamdeset

several nekoliko

sew šiti

shadow sjena

shallow plitak

shame n. sram; stid

shameless bezstidan

share n. súdio

share (stock) akcija

shark morski pas
sharpen zaoštriti
shave v. obriti
she ona
sheep ovca
sheepdog pas ovčar
sheet plahta
shell školjka
shine v. blistati
shirt košulja
shiver v. drhtati
shoe cipela
shoot pucati
shooting pucanje
shop v. kupovati
short kratak
shortage nedostatak
shorten skratiti
shoulder rame
shout v. vikati
show v. pokazati
shower n. tuš
shower (rain) n. pljusak
shy sramežljiv
sick bolestan
side strana
sidewalk pločnik
sight vidik
sign znak
signature podpis
silence tišina
silk svila
silver srebro

similar sličan
simple jednostavan
simply jednostavno
sin n. grijeh
sin v. griješiti
since od
sincere čestit; iskren
sing v. pjevati
sink tonuti
sister sestra
sister-in-law jetrva (brother's wife); zaova
(husband's sister)
sit v. sjediti
situation okolnost
six šest
sixteen šesnaest
sixty šezdeset
size veličina
ski n. skija
ski v. skijati se
skill umijeće
skin koža
skirt haljina
skull lubanja
slap pljeska
sleep v. spavati
sleeping car spavaća kola
sleeve rukav
slim mršav
slogan geslo
Slovakia Slovačka
small sitan; malen
smaller sitniji; manji

smart mudar
smell n. miris; zadah
smile n. smješak
smoke n. dim
smoke v. dimiti
smoked fish odimljena riba
smoker pušač
smooth gladak
snack bar bufet
snake zmija
snore v. hrkati
snow n. snijeg
snow v. sniježiti
so tako
soap sapun
soccer nogomet
society društvo
socks čarape
soft mekan
soldier bojevnik
solitude samoća
some neki
somehow nekako
some kind neka vrsta
someone netko
something nešto
sometime ponekad
somewhere negdje
son sin
song pjesma
son-in-law zet
soon uskoro
sooner skorije

sorrow žalost
sorry žao mi je
soul duša
soup juha
sour kiseo
sour cherry višnja
south jug
southern južni
spark iskra
sparrow vrabac
special osobit
speech govor
speed n. brzina
spell v. slovkati
spend v. potrošiti
spice merodije
spill v. prosuti
spinach špinat
spirit duh
spiritual duševni
spleen slezena
spoil v. pokvariti
spoon žlica
sport šport
spring proljeće
spy špijun
square četvero uglast
squirrel vjeverica
stab v. ubosti
stain mrlja
stair stuba
staircase stepenište
stamp n. pečat; marka

stand v. stajati
standard običan
star zvjezda
starch škrob
startled poplašen
state država
station postaja
statue kip
stay v. ostati
steal v. ukrasti
steam para
steel željezo
step korak
stepfather očuh
stepmother mačeha
stew gulaš
still još
sting ujesti; ubosti
stink v. smrditi
stir mješati
stomach želudac
stone kamen
stop v. zaustaviti
store prodavaona
stork roda
storm oluja
story priča
stove štednjak
straight právó
strange čudan
straw slamka
strawberry jagoda
stream potok

street ulica
strengthen ojačati
stress napetost
strict dosljedan
strike štrajk
striped razgoljen
strong (physically) jak
student student
study n. učenje
study v. učiti
stuffing punjenje
stuffy zadušno
stupid glup
stutter múcati
subject predmet
substitute n. zamjena
suburb predgrađe
success uspjeh
sudden nenadno
suffer trpjeti
sugar šećer
suicide samoubistvo
suit n. odjelo
suitcase kofer
summer ljeto
summon v. sazvati
sun sunce
sunbathe sunčanje
Sunday nedjelja
sunglasses sunčane naočale
sunny sunčano
sunstroke sunčanica
supper večera

supplementary dopunjujući
support v. podupirati
suppose pretpostaviti
surely sigurno
surface površina
surgeon kirurg
surprise v. iznenaditi
suspicious nepovjerljiv
swallow n. lastavica; gutljaj
swallow v. progutati
swear v. zakleti se
sweat znoj
sweater đemper
sweat suit trenerka
sweets slatkiši
swell n. oteklina
swell v. nabreknuti
swim plivati
swimming pool bazen za kupanje
swimsuit kupaći kostim
switch on lights upaliti svjetlo
symphony filharmonija

T

table stol
take v. uzeti
take apart rastaviti
take away odnijeti
take care of oneself brinuti o sebi
tale priča
talent umijeće

talk (long) razgovor

talk v. govoriti

tangerine mandarinka

tape recorder magnetofon

taste okus

taste (style) ukus

tasty ukusno

tax n. porez; taksa

taxi taksi

tea čaj

teach v. učiti

teacher učitelj (m.); čiteljica (f.)

tear n. suza

tedious work dosadan posao

tee shirt majica

telephone brzoglas/telefon

television televizor

temperature toplina

temporarily privremeno

ten deset

tenderness nježnost

tent šator

tenth deseti

terrible grozan

territory predio

terror nasilje

testify svjedočiti

thank v. zahvaliti

thankful zahvalan

thanks hvala

that taj (m.); ta (f.); to (nt.)

theater kazalište
theft krađa
their njihov
then onda
there tamo
therefore radi toga
there isn't any nema nijedan
they oni
thick debeo (m.); debela (f.)
thigh stegno
thin tanak
thing stvar
think v. misliti
third treći
thirst žeđ
thirsty žedan
thirteen trinaest
thirty trideset
this ovaj (m.); ova (f.); ovo (nt.)
this time ovaj put
this way ovuda
thousand tisuća
three tri (m.); tri (f.); troje (nt.)
throat grlo
through kroz
throw v. baciti
thunder grmljavina
Thursday četvrtak
ticket vozna karta
tickle v. škakljati
tie kravata
tight tjesan

time (era) doba
timely u vrijeme
tip (money) napojnica
tip (point) oštrica
tired umoran
toast dvopek; zdravica
today danas
together zajedno
toilet zahod
tolerant obziran
tomato rajčica
tomorrow sutra
too također
tooth zub
toothpick čačkalica
torture n. mučenje
torture v. mučiti
tourist turist
toward k; ka
tower toranj
town grad
toy igračka
track and field atletika
trackless trolley trolejbus
tradition predaja
traffic promet
train n. vlak
trained izučen
trait osobina
traitor izdajnik
translation prevod
transport v. prevoziti

transportation prevoz
travel n. putovanje
tray poslužavnik
treat v. liječiti
tree stablo
trip n. putovanje
trousers hlače
trout pastrva
true istinito
truly stvarno
trumpet truba
truth istina
try v. pokušati
Tuesday utorak
turkey puran
Turkey Turska
turn zaokret
turn out izvratit
turn over preokrenut
twelfth dvanaesti
twelve dvanaest
twenty dvadeset
twins blizanci
two dva (m.); dvije (f.); dvoje (nt.)
type uzorak

U

ugly ružan
ulcer čir
umbrella kišobran

unbelievable nevjerovatan
uncertain neizvjestan
uncle stric (father's brother); ujak (mother's brother)
uncomfortable neudoban
unconsciousness nesvjest
under ispod
understand (a concept) proniknut
understand (speech) razumjeti
underwear veš
undress svući
unemployed nezaposlen
unfold odmotati
unfortunately nažalost
unhealthy nezdrav
uninteresting nezanimljiv
unite v. sjediniti
United States Sjedinjene Države
universe svemir
university univerzitet
unjust nepravedan
unknown nepoznat
unlawful nezakonit
unnecessary nepotrebno
unrest nemir
up góré
upper gornji
urine mokrača
use n. upotreba
use v. uživati; upotrebiti
use (drug) trošiti droge
useless nekoristan
utilize iskoristiti

V

vacation praznici
vacuum cleaner usisavač prašine
valley dolina
value n. vrijednost
value v. cjeniti
variety raznovrsnost
various raznovrstan
veal teletina
vegetable povrće
vehicle vozilo
vein vena
very vrlo
victory pobjeda
vile zao; podlac
village selo
violin vijolina
virtue čestitost
visa viza
visit v. posjetiti
voice glas
volleyball odbojka
volunteer dragovoljac
vote n. glasanje
vote v. glasati

W

wage klin
wagon vagon
wait v. čekati

waiter konobar
waitress konobarica
wake up probuditi
walk v. hodati
wall zid
wander v. lutati
want v. htjeti
war n. rat
wardrobe haljine
warm topao
warm up zagrijati
warning opomena; pozor
wash (by hand) prati (na ruke)
washing machine mašina za pranje
wasp osa
waste v. rasipat
waste of time gubljenje vremena
watch (guard) stražar
watch v. čuvati
watch over pričuvati
water voda
waterfall vodopad
watermelon dinja
we mi (pl.)
weak slab
weakness slabost
weapon oružje
weather vrijeme
weave tkati
wedding svadba
Wednesday srijeda
week tjedan
weekend konac tjedna

weight n. težina
weigh v. vagati
welcome dobro došli
well (water) bunar
west zapad
western zapadni
wet adj. mokar
whale kit
what što
whatever bilo što
what for zašto
what kind koje vrste
wheel kotač
when kad
whenever bilo kad
where gdje
wherever bilo gdje
which koji
whichever bilo koji
whisper v. šaptati
whistle v. zviždati
white bjelo
white man bjelac
who tko
whoever bilo tko
whole sav; cjeli
whose čiji (m.); čija (f.); čije (nt.)
why zašto
wide širok
widow udovica
widower udovac
width širina
wife supruga; žena

wild divlji
will n. volja
willingness spremnost
win v. pobjediti
wind vjetar
window prozor
wine vino
wing krilo
winter zima
wintry ziman
wise man mudrac
wish n. želja
wish v. željeti
with s; sa
without bez
witness svjedok
wolf vuk
woman žena
wonder čuđenje
wonderful izvanredan
wood drvo
wool vuna
word riječ
work n. rad
work v. raditi
workday radni dan
worker radnik
workroom radna soba
workshop radiona
world svijet
worldly svjetski
worry v. brigati se
worse najgori

worsen pogoršati
wrap up v. zamotati
wrinkle n. bora
wrist ručni zglob
write pisati
writer pisac; književnik
wrong adj. nepravedan
wrong n. nepravda

X

x-rays rentgensko zračenje

Y

yard obor; dvorište
yawn v. zjevati
year godina
yearly godišnje
yellow žuto
yes da
yesterday jučer
yet još
yolk žumance
you (for.) vi
you (infor.) ti
young mlad
younger mlađi
youngest najmlađi
your (for.) vaš (m.); vaša (f.); vaše (nt.)
your (infor.) tvoj (m.); tvoja (f.); tvoje (nt.)
youth mladost

Z

zeal predanost
zebra zebra
zero nula
zest slast
zinc cink
zone zona
zoo zoološki vrt
zoology zoologija

CROATIAN PHRASEBOOK

1. QUICK REFERENCE

Hi!	**Halo!**
How are you?	**Kako si? (infor.)**
	Kako ste? (for.)
Good, thank you.	**Hvala, dobro.**
Good morning!	**Dobro jutro!**
Good day.	**Dobar dan.**
Good evening.	**Dobra večer**.
Good night.	**Laku noć.**
Till tomorrow.	**Do sutra.**
Good-bye!	**Do viđenja!**
Good luck!	**Sa srećom!**
	Sretno!
I wish you a good journey.	**Želim vam sretan put.**
All the best!	**Sve najbolje!**
Welcome!	**Dobro došao (m.)**
	Došla! (f.)
Bon appétit!	**Prijatno!**
Please.	**Molim.**
Thank you.	**Hvala.**
Excuse me.	**Oprostite mi.**
Could I?	**Da li mogu?**
I am sorry.	**Vrlo mi je žao.**
yes	**da**
no	**ne**
What?	**Što?**
What is that?	**Što je to?**
What does that mean?	**Što to znači?**

Who?	**Tko?**
Who is that?	**Tko je to?**
Why?	**Zašto?**
because	**zato**
That's the way it is!	**To je tako!**
Good!	**Dobro!**
Bad!	**Loše!**
Can you tell me, please?	**Možete mi reći, molim?**
How do you write this?	**Kako se ovo piše?**
Help me!	**Pomozite mi, molim!**
Is that right?	**Da li je to ispravno?**
Be so kind.	**Budite ljubazan. (m.)**
	Budite ljubazna. (f.)
Where?	**Gdje?**
Where to?	**Kamo?**
When?	**Kad?**
How?	**Kako?**
How far?	**Kako daleko?**
How long?	**Kako dugo?**
How much?	**Koliko košta?**
Is it close?	**Jeli blizu?**
here	**tu**
there	**tamo**
I can't.	**Nemogu.**
I want to...	**Hoću...**
...rest.	**...počivat.**
...eat.	**...jesti.**
...drink.	**...piti.**
...sleep.	**...spavati.**
Which one?	**Koji? (m.)**
	Koja? (f.)

I	**Ja**
you	**ti (infor.), vi (for.)**
he	**on**
she	**ona**
it	**ono**
we	**mi**
they	**oni**

I like it.	**Ja to volim.**
I do not like it.	**Ja to nevolim.**
I want...	**Ja hoće...**
I do not want...	**Ja neću...**
I know.	**Ja znam.**
I do not know.	**Je neznam.**
You do not understand.	**Vi ne razumjete.**
I am sorry to hear that.	**Žao mi je to čuti.**
I am grateful.	**Zahvalan sam. (m.)**
	Zahvalna sam. (f.)

This is important.	**Ovo je važno.**
It does not matter.	**Ništa zato.**
It is nothing.	**Nije ništa.**
No problem.	**Nema problema.**
Here it is.	**Ovdje je. Evo ga.**
Here they are.	**Tu su. Evo ih.**
this	**ovaj (m.), ova (f.),**
	ovo (nt.)
these	**ovi**
Everything is fine.	**Sve je u redu.**
Danger!	**Opasnost!**

I am cold.	**Hladno mi je.**
I am hot.	**Meni je vruće.**
I am fine.	**Ja sam dobro.**

Croatian-English Dictionary and Phrasebook • 175

I am tired.	**Ja sam umoran. (m.)**
	Ja sam umorna. (f.)
I am sleepy.	**Ja sam pospan. (m.)**
	Ja sam pospana. (f.)
I am hungry.	**Ja sam gladan. (m.)**
	Ja sam gladna. (f.)
I am thirsty.	**Ja sam žedan. (m.)**
	Ja sam žedna. (f.)
I am glad.	**Ja sam radostan. (m.)**
	Ja sam radosna. (f.)
I am sad.	**Ja sam žalostan. (m.)**
	Ja sam žalosna. (f.)
I am surprised.	**Ja sam iznenađen. (m.)**
	Ja sam iznenađena. (f.)

Adjectives - Pridjevi

angry	**ljutit/a (m./f.)**
big	**velik/a (m./f.)**
bright	**blistav/a (m./f.)**
colorful	**šarolik/a (m./f.)**
dim	**blijedo**
dry	**suh/a (m./f.)**
fat	**debeo (m.)/debela (f.)**
happy	**sretan (m.)/sretna (f.)**
hard	**tvrd/a (m./f.)**
long	**dúg/a (m./f.)**
low	**nizak (m.)/niska (f.)**
moist	**vlažan (m.)/vlažna (f.)**
narrow	**uzak (m.)/uska (f.)**

poor	**siromašan (m.)/ siromašna (f.)**
pretty	**lijep/a (m./f.)**
rich	**bogat/a (m./f.)**
sad	**tužan (m.)/tužna (f.)**
short	**kratak (m.)/kratka (f.)**
slim	**mršav/a (m./f.)**
small	**sitan (m.)/sitna (f.)**
smart	**pametan/a (m./f.)**
soft	**mekan/a (m./f.)**
sticky	**ljepljiv/a (m./f.)**
stupid	**budalast/a (m./f.)**
tall	**stasit/a (m./f.)**
tasty	**ukusno**
ugly	**ružan (m.)/ružna (f.)**
wet	**mokar (m.)/mokra (f.)**
wide	**širok/a (m./f.)**

2. FAMILY

family	**obitelj**
relatives	**rodbina**
children	**djeca**
adults	**odrasli**
wife, spouse	**žena, supruga**
husband, spouse	**čovjek, suprug**
mother	**majka, mater**
father	**otac**
baby	**djete**
daughter	**kćer**
son	**sin**
sister	**sestra**
brother	**brat**
grandmother	**baka, baba**
grandfather	**djed**
granddaughter	**unuka**
grandson	**unuk**
aunt	**teta, tetka**
uncle	**stric (father's brother) ujak (mother's brother)**
niece	**nećaka**
nephew	**sinovac (brother's son) sestrić (sister's son)**
cousin	**rođak (m.), rodica (f.)**
mother-in-law	**svekrva (husband's mother)**
mother-in-law	**punica, tašta (wife's mother)**
father-in-law	**svekar (husband's father)**

father-in-law	**punac, tast (wife's father)**
brother-in-law	**badženak, šogor (wife's brother)**
brother-in-law	**djever (husband's brother)**
sister-in-law	**jetrva (husband's brother's wife)**
sister-in-law	**zaova (husband's sister)**

3. INTRODUCTIONS

Introductions	**Upoznavanje**
My name is...	**Moje ime je...**
Pleased to meet you.	**Drago mi je da smo se upoznali.**
May I introduce...	**Mogu vam predstaviti...**
my husband.	**moj muž/suprug.**
my wife.	**moja žena/supruga.**
my friend.	**moj prijatelj.**
my family.	**moja obitelj.**
my acquaintance.	**moj znanac.**
Where are you from?	**Odkud ste?**
I am from...	**Ja sam iz...**
America.	**Amerike.**
Canada.	**Kanade.**
England.	**Engleske.**
What is your nationality?	**Koje ste nardnosti?**
I am...	**Ja sam...**
American.	**Amerikanac. (m.)**
	Amerikanka. (f.)
Canadian.	**Kanađanin. (m.)**
	Kanađanka. (f.)
British.	**Englez. (m.)**
	Engleskinja. (f.)
What are you doing?	**Što radiš?**
Here?	**Ovdje?**
I am a tourist.	**Ja sam turist.**
I am studying here.	**Ja ovdje studiram.**
I am here on business.	**Ja sam tu poslovno.**
What is your profession?	**Što je vaša profesija?**
I am a...	**Ja sam...**

artist.	**umjetnik. (m.)**
	umjetnica. (f.)
businessman.	**trgovački putnik.**
doctor.	**doktor. (m.)**
	doktorica. (f.)
engineer.	**inžinjer.**
housewife.	**kućanica.**
journalist.	**reporter.**
lawyer.	**advokat.**
musician.	**muzikant. (m.)**
	muzikantkinja. (f.)
nurse.	**medicinska sestra.**
politician.	**političar. (m.)**
	političarka. (f.)
scientist.	**učenjak. (m.)**
	učenjakinja. (f.)
soldier.	**bojevnik, vojnik.**
student.	**student. (m.)**
	studentica. (f.)
teacher.	**učitelj. (m.)**
	učiteljica. (f.)
writer.	**književnik.**
How long have you been here?	**Kako dugo ste ovdje?**
I have been here...	**Ja sam ovdje...**
a day.	**dan.**
a week.	**tjedan.**
a month.	**mjesec dana.**
Do you like it here?	**Da li vam se sviđa ovdje?**
Yes, very much.	**Da, vrlo mnogo.**
No, not at all.	**Ne, nimalo.**

I am having a great time.	**Ja tu stvarno uživam.**
Where are you staying?	**Gdje vi odsjedate?**
At the hotel.	**U hotelu.**
Are you married?	**Da li ste oženjen? (m.)**
	Da li ste udata? (f.)
Yes, I am.	**Da, jesam.**
No, I am not.	**Ne, nisam.**
Do you have children?	**Imate li djece?**

4. BASIC CONVERSATIONAL EXPRESSONS

Do you speak…	**Dali govorite….**
English?	**Engleski?**
Croatian?	**Hrvatski?**
German?	**Njemački?**
French?	**Francuski?**
Spanish?	**Španjolski?**
Does someone here speak English?	**Da li metko ovdje govori Engleski?**
Only a little.	**Samo malo.**
Not at all.	**Nimalo.**
I can understand, but I don't speak it.	**Razumijem, ali ne govorim.**
Do you understand?	**Razumjete li ?**
I don't understand.	**Ne razumjem.**
Please, speak more slowly.	**Molim vas govorite sporije.**
Please repeat that.	**Molim vas, ponovite to.**
Please, write it down.	**Molim vas napišite to.**
Translate.	**Prevedite mi.**
What does this mean?	**Što to znači?**
What did he/she say?	**Što je on rekao (m.)/ ona rekla (f.)?**

5. CUSTOMS

customs	**carinarnica**
passport	**pasoš**
Your passport, please.	**Vaš pasoš, molim.**
Here it is.	**Evo ga.**
Please wait till I find it.	**Molim vas, pričekajte dok to nađem.**
How long are you staying?	**Kako dugo ćete ostati?**
A few days.	**Nekoliko dana.**
A week.	**Tjedan dana.**
Two weeks.	**Dva tjedna.**
A month.	**Mjesec dana.**
family name	**prezime**
first name	**krstno ime**
address	**adresa**
date of birth	**datum rođenja**
place of birth	**mjesto rođenja**
nationality	**narodnost**
age	**starost**
occupation	**zanimanje**
sex	**spol**
religion	**vjeroispovjest; vjera**
purpose of travel	**svrha putovanja**
date of arrival	**datum dolaska**
date of departure	**datum odlaska**
passport number	**broj pasoša; putnice**
Have you anything to declare?	**Imate li nešto da prijavite?**
Open this suitcase.	**Otvorite ovaj kofer.**
What is this?	**Što je ovo?**

You have to pay duty on this.	**Na ovo trebate platit carinu.**
It is for my personal use.	**Ovo je za moju osobnu upotrebu.**
It is a gift.	**To je dar.**
It is not new.	**To nije novo.**
Do you have more luggage?	**Da li imate još putne spreme?**
Is that all?	**Jeli to sve?**
I have...	**Ja imam...**
cigarettes.	**cigareta.**
a bottle of wine.	**flašu vina.**
a bottle of brandy.	**flašu rakije.**
I don't understand.	**Ja ne razumijem.**
Does anyone here speak English?	**Da li itko ovdje govori Engleski?**
baggage	**putna sprema**
porter	**nosač**
Please carry my bag.	**Molim vas ponesite moj kofer.**
That is mine.	**To je moje.**
Take these things to...	**Odnesite ove stvari...**
the bus.	**na autobus.**
the taxi.	**do taksija.**
How much do I owe you?	**Koliko vam trebam platiti?**
My luggage is lost.	**Moja putna sprema se izgubila.**

6. CAR RENTAL

Driving in Croatia is only for those with a spirit of adventure. Cars can be rented at the airport and in a few locations in larger towns, but you must have an international driver's license (which can be obtained at most auto clubs). Gasoline stations are scarce, but with proper planning you should have no problems. Roads are generally in good repair, and suitable maps are available. Road regulations are strictly enforced, and fines must be paid at the point of issue. Driving under the influence is severely punished and if you plan to be drinking, you should not be driving.

car rental	**zakup auta**
I'd like to rent a car.	**Htio bi zakupit auto.**
What is the rate?	**Koliko košta?**
Per day?	**Na dan?**
Per week?	**Na tjedan?**
What is the charge per kilometer?	**Koliko naknadno po kilometru?**
Are the prices of gas and oil included?	**Da li je cjena benzina i ulja uključena?**
I need it for...	**Ja to trebam za...**
a day.	**jedan dan.**
three days.	**tri dana.**
two weeks.	**dva tjedna.**
Here is my...	**Evo moje...**
international driver's license.	**međunarodne vozačke dozvole.**
credit card.	**kreditne karte.**

I am not familiar with this car.	**Nisam upoznat s ovim autom.**
What is this?	**što je ovo?**
Explain this to me.	**Objasnite mi ovo.**
Show me how this mechanism works.	**Pokažite mi kako ovaj mehanizam radi.**
Where can I buy gas?	**Gdje mogu kupiti benzina?**
Do I need anything else?	**Da li trebam išta drugo?**
gas pump	**benzinska pumpa**
service station	**mehanička radnja**
parking lot	**parkiralište**

ACCOMMODATION

7. ACCOMMODATION

It would be wise to make hotel arrangements before you arrive in Croatia. This is especially true if you are visiting the Dalmatian Coast (Split, Dubrovnik) in the busy summer months. Many hotels in this country focus on serving western tourists. A variety of services are usually available at your hotel, depending on its size. The larger ones will have a postal service, currency exchange office, gift shop, restaurant, bar, dry cleaner, laundry, hair salon and barbershop. Also, the hotels usually have an information office (**informacjie**) where the staff knows English.

Check in - Pristup u hotel
Checking in to your hotel is an easy procedure now that Croatia is an independent nation. All you need is your passport with a Croatian visa.

Do you speak English?	**Govorite li Engleski?**
My name is...	**Moje ime je...**
I have a reservation.	**Ja imam rezervaciju.**
Here are my documents.	**Evo mojih isprava.**
I'd like a single/double bedroom.	**Htio bi sobu sa jednim/dva kreveta.**
I'd like a room with a...	**Htio bi sobu s...**
double bed.	**duplim krevetom.**
two twin beds.	**dva dupla kreveta.**
a bath.	**kupaonu.**
a shower.	**tuš.**
a private toilet.	**privatni zahod.**

a telephone.	**sa telefonom.**
a television.	**sa televizorom.**
a balcony.	**sa balkonom.**
a view.	**sa pogledom na.**

Is there…	**Dali imate…**
room service?	**sobnu poslugu?**
a dining room?	**blagovaonu?**
air conditioning?	**klimatizaciju?**
heating?	**grijanje?**
hot water?	**toplu vodu?**
a garage?	**garažu?**

May I see the room?	**Mogu li vidjeti sobu?**
Yes, I'll take it.	**Dobro, uzet ću je.**
No, I don't like it.	**Ne, ne sviđa mi se.**
Do you have anything else?	**Dali imate nešto drugo?**
I asked for a room with a bath.	**Ja sam tražio sobu s kupatilom.**

Registration - Registracija; Upis

Once your reservation has been confirmed, you will be asked to present your passport and fill out a registration form. Your passport may be kept overnight for processing, but you should be able to pick it up the next day. If you plan to exchange money, be sure you do it before you register, since you'll need your passport to carry out the transaction.

accommodation	**u hotelu**
registration form	**upisna forma**

ACCOMMODATION

Fill out this form.	**Ispunite ovu formu.**
Sign here.	**Podpišite ovdje.**
Your passport, please.	**Vaš pasport, molim.**
How long will you be here?	**Kako dugo mislite ovdje ostati?**
What does this mean?	**Što ovo znači?**
What's my room number?	**Koji je broj moje sobe?**
My key, please.	**Moj ključ, molim.**
Take my luggage to my room, please.	**Odnesite moje kofere u moju sobu.**
Is there an elevator?	**Dali imate lift?**

The Staff - Posluga

Beyond language, the Croatian standard is politeness, although you may not realize it from the surly attitude of many in the service industry. Nevertheless, it is a good idea to be polite and friendly to the hotel staff, because they can make your stay much more pleasant.

hall/floor	**predvorje**
doorman	**vratar**
porter	**nosač**
maid	**sobarica**
receptionist	**osoba za primanje**
phone operator	**telefon operator**
waiter	**konobar**
waitress	**konobarica**
manager	**upravitelj; šef**

Questions - Pitanja

The voltage in Croatia is 220 AC. The plugs and sockets are like those used in the western part of Europe, and Americans should bring electrical adapters and converters for their electrical appliances.

Can you please	**Molim vas možete mi**
bring me…	**donijeti…**
a towel?	**ručnik?**
a blanket?	**pokrivač?**
a pillow?	**uzglavnik; jastuk?**
an ashtray?	**pepeljaru?**
some hangers?	**nekoliko vješalica?**
some soap?	**sapun?**
Where are the toilets?	**Gdje je zahod?**
Where is the…	**Gdje je…**
restaurant/bar?	**restoran/bar?**
post office?	**pošta?**
information office?	**ured za informacije?**
hairdresser?	**frizer (m.)?**
	frizerka (f.)?
barber?	**brico?**
currency exchange?	**mjenjačnica novca?**
office?	**ured?**
light switch?	**električni upaljač?**
electrical outlet?	**električni priključak?**

Problems - Nezgode

You should be aware that hot water is not always available. It is advisable to ask about this matter during check-in.

air conditioning	**klimatizacija**
electrical outlet	**električni utikač**
fan	**ventilatora**
faucet	**slavina**
heating	**grijanje**
lamp	**sijalice**
light	**svjetla**
radio	**radio**
shower	**tuš**
telephone	**telefon; brzoglas**
television	**televizor**
toilet	**zahod**
(hot) water	**(vruće) vode**

The… does not work.	**Ovo... ne radi.**
There is no…	**Tu nema...**
The sink is clogged.	**Umivaonik je začepljen.**
The door/window is jammed.	**Vrata/prozor se neda otvoriti.**
The door does not lock.	**Vrata se nemogu zaključati.**
Can it be repaired?	**Dali se to može popraviti?**
checkout	**odlazak**
I am leaving today.	**Ja odlazim danas.**
Please prepare my bill.	**Molim vas pripremite moj račun; dûg.**
Do you accept credit cards?	**Dali mogu platit kreditnom kartom?**
I think there is a mistake.	**Mislim, da je tu mala greška.**

Could you please send someone to get my bags?	**Molim vas možete poslat nekoga da donese moje kofere?**
Where can I get a cab?	**Gdje mogu naručit taksi?**

8. FOOD & DRINK

Eating out can be fun, but do not expect it to be like it is in the West. Restaurants are generally inexpensive, with the exception of some of the regional dining establishments. Usually, the restaurant staffs are not known for their eagerness to please, and service can be quite slow. Do not be surprised to be seated at a table with people you do not know (it is a common practice in Central and Eastern Europe). Dishes that do not have prices on the menu are priced by weight or season. Special orders or changes to menu items could result in extremely long waits. Payment is made to the headwaiter at the end of the meal. Tips are generally included in the bill.

Types of Establishments - Vrste Lokala

Restauracija—Restaurants usually have a wide variety of dishes, reservations are strongly recommended, and closing time is usually 11:00 P.M.

Dietna Restauracija—Dietetic restaurants specialize in satisfying special needs (low fat, no salt, vegetarian meals).

Kavana—Cafes that offer a limited menu, but provide music and dancing. Customers often arrive early and spend the evening.

Bufet—Inexpensive, limited menu, stand-up "fast-food" style establishments.

Slastičarna—Coffee shop serving a variety of sweets and ice cream.

Sladoled—Ice cream/soft drink shop.
Vinski Podrum—Wine cellar serving a wide
variety of wines and a limited snack menu.
Krčma—Working man's drinking establishment.

The Preliminaries - Uputstva

food and drink	**hrana I pića**
I'm hungry.	**Ja sam gladan. (m.)**
	Ja sam gladna. (f.)
I'd like to eat/drink.	**Ja bi htio jesti/piti.**
Can you recommend a good restaurant?	**Možete li preporučiti dobru restauraciju?**
Do you serve breakfast/ lunch/dinner?	**Dali servirate doručak/ručak/ večeru?**
I'd like to make a reservation.	**Htio bi (m.)/Htjela bi (f.) napravit rezervaciju.**
There will be 2/3/4 of us.	**Ima nas 2/3/4.**
We will arrive at six.	**Doći ćemo u šest sati.**
Where is the coatroom?	**Gdje je garderoba?**
Coat check number	**Broj za kaput molim**
Where are the bathrooms?	**Gdje je zahod?**
Is this place...	**Dali je ovo mjesto...**
taken?	**zauzeto?**
reserved?	**rezervirano?**
free?	**slobodno?**
Have a seat!	**Sjednite!**
We prefer a table...	**Volili bi stol...**
in the corner.	**u ćošku.**
by the window.	**pri prozoru.**
outside.	**vani.**

May we have another table?	**Možemo li dobiti jedan drugi stol?**
Is smoking permitted here?	**Dali je ovdje dozvoljeno pušenje?**

Ordering - Narudžba

This way, please.	**Ovamo, molim.**
May I have a menu, please?	**Dali mogu dobit jelovnik, molim?**
Have you decided?	**Dali ste se odlučili?**
What do you recommend?	**Što vi preporučate?**
Unfortunately, we do not have...	**Oprostit ćete ali nemamo...**
Why not take this instead?	**Zašto nebi uzeli ovo umjesto?**
What would you like?	**Što bi vi želili?**
Go ahead.	**Donesite.**
I'll have...	**Ja bi htio (m.)...**
	Ja bi htjela (f.)...
for an appetizer.	**za predjelo.**
for the main course.	**za glavno jelo.**
for dessert.	**završno jelo; kolače.**
a small portion.	**malu porciju.**
What would you like to drink?	**Hoćete nešto piti?**
I recommend...	**Ja preporučam...**
That's all, thank you.	**To je sve hvala lijepo.**

The Meal - Jelo

Enjoy your meal!	**Prijatno!**
How is it?	**Jeli dobro?**
It's very tasty.	**Vrlo je ukusno.**
Please pass me...	**Molim, dajte mi...**
a cup.	**šalicu.**

a glass.	**čašu.**
a fork.	**viljušku.**
a knife.	**nož.**
a spoon.	**žlicu.**
a plate.	**tanjur.**
a napkin.	**salvetu.**
an ashtray.	**pepeljaru.**
some salt.	**malo soli.**
some pepper.	**malo papra.**
sugar.	**šećera.**
water.	**vode.**
bread and butter.	**kruha i putra.**
Can I have some more of this?	**Bi li mogao (m.)/ mogla (f.) imati još malo toga?**

Complaints - Prigovori

I have a complaint.	**Imam prigovor.**
This is…	**Ovo je...**
cold.	**hladno.**
hot.	**vruće.**
too spicy.	**previše papreno.**
too sweet/salty.	**preslatko/preslano.**
sour.	**kiselo.**
stale.	**pokvareno.**
overdone.	**prepečeno.**
underdone.	**nedokuhano.**
This is dirty.	**Ovo je nečisto.**
I don't like this.	**Nevolim ovo.**
You can take this away.	**Možete ovo pospremiti.**
This isn't what I ordered.	**Ovo nije što sam naručio (m.)/ naručila (f.).**

I ordered….	**Ja sam naručio (m.)/ naručila (f.)…**
I don't want it.	**Ja to neću.**

The Check - Račun

Tipping is appreciated and often expected when serving foreigners. Between ten and fifteen percent is about average for waiters. More than extra money, people welcome small gifts and souvenirs. Croatians are very hospitable and like to make presents for close family and friends. Typical presents are needlework or handcrafts.

We've finished.	**Dovršili smo.**
I have had enough.	**Bilo mi je dosta.**
Bring me the check, please.	**Dajte mi račun, molim.**
There's been a mistake.	**Izgleda mi da je greška.**
How did you get this total?	**Kako ste došli do ove cifre?**
Is a tip included?	**Dali ste uračunali napojnicu?**
Pay the cashier.	**Platite na blagajni.**
We'd like to pay separately.	**Htjeli bi platit zasebno.**
Do you accept…	**Dali primate…**
traveler's checks?	**travel čekove?**
credit cards?	**kreditne karte?**
Thank you, this is for you.	**Hvala lijepo, ovo je za vas.**

Snack Bars and Cafeterias - Bufet I Kafići

At Croatian snack bars, just like in the United States, you usually pick up what you want, or else ask someone behind the counter for it. Be sure to carry small bills with you because the cashiers very often will not accept anything larger than a twenty kuna note.

What's this?	**Što je to?**
Please give me one of those.	**Dajte mi jedan od ovih, molim.**
I'd like that, please.	**Ja bi hitio (m.)/ htjela (f.) to, molim.**
Please give me a piece of that.	**Molim vas dajte mi dio toga.**
May I help myself?	**Mogu li se poslužiti sam (m.)/sama (f.)?**
Just a little.	**Samo malo.**
A little more, please.	**Malo više, molim.**
Enough?	**Dosta?**
Anything else?	**Još nešto?**
That's all, thank you.	**To je sve, hvala.**
How much is it?	**Koliko košta?**
Is that to go?	**Da li je to za ponijet sa sobom?**

Food - Jela

The main thing to keep in mind with regard to the various foods and drinks listed in this chapter is their limited availability. Not everything will be available everywhere you go, so be prepared to experience new foods and methods of preparation. Most Croatian national dishes are quite good.

Breakfast - Doručak

Where can I have breakfast?	**Gdje mogu doručkovat?**
What time is breakfast served?	**U koje vrijeme se servira doručak?**
How long is breakfast served?	**Do koje dobi se servira doručak?**
I'd like…	**Htio bi (m.)…**
	Hjela bi (f.)…
(black) coffee.	**(crnu) kavu.**
with milk.	**sa mlijekom.**
with sugar.	**sa šećerom.**
without sugar.	**bez šećera.**
tea.	**čaj.**
with lemon.	**sa limunom.**
with milk.	**sa mlijekom.**
with honey.	**sa medom.**
with sugar.	**sa šećerom.**
cocoa.	**kokao.**
milk.	**mlijeko.**
orange juice.	**narančada.**
apple juice.	**jabučni sok.**
yogurt.	**jogurt.**
bread.	**kruh.**
toast.	**dvopek.**
a roll.	**žemičku.**
butter.	**putar.**
cheese.	**sir.**
jam.	**džem.**
honey.	**med.**
oatmeal.	**kaša.**
grits.	**orzo.**
eggs.	**jaja.**

scrambled eggs.	pofrigana.
sunny-side up.	jaja na oko.
soft-boiled eggs.	u sorbulu.
hard-boiled eggs.	jaja u tvrdo.
salt/pepper.	so/papar.

Appetizers - Predjela

For an appetizer I want...	Za predjelo htio bi (m.)/ htjela bi (f.)...
(black/red) caviar.	(crni/crveni) kaviar.
cheese.	sir.
cucumber salad.	salata od krastavaca.
ham.	pršut.
meat.	meso.
meat/fish plate.	meso/riba.
pickles.	kiseli krastavci.
potato salad.	krompir salata.
salad.	salata.
sauerkraut.	kiseli kupus.
sardines.	sardine.
sweet cabbage.	slatki kupus.
tomato salad.	salata od rajčica.

Soups - Juhe

Please bring me some...	Molim donesite mi malo...
beef broth.	govedske juhe.
cabbage soup.	juhu od kupusa.
chicken broth.	pileće juhe.
chicken soup.	pileće juhe.
with noodles.	s rezancima.
with rice.	s rižom.
fish soup.	riblja juha.

lentil soup.	**juhu od leće.**
mushroom soup.	**juhu od gljiva.**
pea soup.	**juhu od biži.**
potato soup.	**juhu od krompira.**
vegetable soup.	**juha od povrća.**

Side Dishes - Pomoćna Jela

I'd like…	**Htio bi (m.)…**
	Htjela bi (f.)…
baked.	**pečenih.**
boiled.	**kuhanih.**
french fries.	**frenč frajz.**
fried.	**friganih.**
mashed.	**pire krompir.**
pasta.	**tjestenine.**
potatoes.	**krompira.**
rice.	**riže.**

Vegetables - Povrće

What kind of vegetables do you have?	**Kakvu vrstu povrća imate?**
beets	**cikle**
cabbage	**kupusa**
red cabbage	**crvenog kupusa**
carrots	**mrkva**
corn	**kukuruz**
cucumbers	**krastavaca**
green beans	**zelene mahune**
leeks	**poriluk**
mushrooms	**gljiva/pečurke**
onions	**luk-crveni**
peas	**biži**

potatoes	**krompira**
radishes	**rotkvica**
tomatoes	**rajčica**
wax beans	**žute mahune**

blueberries	**borovice**
cherries	**trešnje**
currants	**ribizl**
dates	**datulje**
figs	**smokve**
lemon	**limun**
prunes	**suhe šljive**
raisins	**suho grožđe**
raspberries	**maline**
sour cherry	**višnje**
strawberries	**jagode**
wild strawberries	**šumske jagode**

Desserts - Slatkiši/Desert

cake	**torta**
chocolate	**čokolada**
cookie	**keks**
crepe with jam	**palačinke**
doughnut	**krofne**
ice cream	**sladoled**
pastry	**kolači**
pudding	**puding**
stewed fruit	**kompot**

Drinks - Pića

Coffee and tea are very popular. Coffee is very strong and good, but it is expensive. Tea is usually served presweetened with honey, jam, or sugar.

Bottled fruit juices and waters are also very popular, but iced and cold drinks are not.

What do you have to drink?	**Što imate za piti?**
Please bring me...	**Molim vas donesite...**
(black) coffee.	**(crna) kave.**
with milk.	**s mliekom.**
with sugar.	**s šećerom.**
without sugar.	**bez šećera.**
tea.	**čaj.**
with lemon.	**s limunom.**
with milk.	**s mliekom.**
with honey.	**s medom.**
water.	**voda.**
a soft drink.	**soda.**
I'd like a glass of...	**Htio (m.)/Htjela bi (f.) čašu...**
milk.	**mlieka.**
lemonade.	**limunade.**
I'd like a bottle of	**Htio bi flašu**
mineral water.	**mineralne vode.**
I'd like a bottle of...	**Htio bi flašu ...**
juice.	**soka.**
apple	**jabukova**
cherry	**trešnjina**
grape	**grožđena**
orange	**narančina**

Alcoholic Drink - Alkoholna Pića

The most popular wines in Croatia come from Istria and Dalmatia. Plum brandy (Sljivovca) is the most popular drink. Dalmatian cherry liquor (Maraskino) is a unique treat that should be experienced. Beer is served with meals in Northern Croatia.

Do you serve alcohol?	**Dali prodajete alkoholno piće?**
Which wine would you recommend?	**Koje vino preporučate?**
How much is a bottle?	**Koliko košta flaša?**
I'd like a glass/bottle of wine.	**Htio bi čašu/flašu vina.**
red wine	**cervenog vina**
white wine	**bjelog vina**
sweet wine	**slatkog vina**
champagne	**šampanjca**
beer	**piva**
plum brandy	**šljivovice**
whiskey (straight)	**viski**
with ice	**sa ledom**
with soda	**sa sodom**
cognac	**konjak**
rum	**rum**

Toasts - Zdravice

To your health!	**Na zdravlje!**
Congratulations!	**Čestitam vam!**
I wish you...	**Želim vam...**
happiness!	**sreću!**
health!	**zdravlje!**
success!	**uspjeh!**

9. MONEY/FINANCE

money; currency	**novac**
Where can I change some money?	**Gdje mogu da razmjenim novac?**
I'd like to change some dollars.	**Htio bi razmjenit nešto dolara.**
Can you cash these traveler's checks?	**Možete mi razmjenit ove travel čekove?**
What is the exchange rate?	**Kolika je rata razmjene?**
Can you give me smaller bills?	**Možete mi dati manjih novčanica?**

Currency Exchange - Razmjena novca

If you do not exchange your money upon arrival at the airport or in your hotel, you may also exchange it at exchange offices or banks. Be forewarned that they are less common than in the West.

Where can I exchange money?	**Gdje mogu da razmjenim novac?**
When does the bank open?	**Kad se otvara banka?**
How late is the bank open?	**Kako dugo je banka otvorena?**
The bank is open from 9:30 A.M. to 1:00 P.M.	**Banka je otvorena od 9:30 do 13:00 sati popodne.**
What is the exchange rate for dollars (today)?	**Kolika je rata razmjene za dolare (danas)?**

I'd like to cash some traveler's checks.	**Htio bi (m.)/Htjela bi (f.) razmjenit nekoliko travel čekova.**
Can I purchase an international money order here?	**Mogu li tu kupit međunarodnu novčanu uputnicu?**
What is the charge?	**Koliko dugujem za uslugu?**
I'm expecting money from America.	**Očekujem novac iz Amerike.**
Has it arrived?	**Dali je došao?**
Go to the cashier's office.	**Idite u ofis kod blagajnika.**
Where is the cashier's office?	**Gdje je blagajna?**
When is the cashier open?	**Kad je blagajna otvorena?**
Are you the cashier?	**Dali ste vi blagajnik (m.)/blagajnica (f.)?**
Here's my identification.	**Evo mojih osobnih isprava.**
Where do I sign?	**Gdje da se potpišem?**
May I please have large/small bills?	**Molim vas mogu li da dobijem krupnije/ sitnije novčanice?**
Can you give me small change?	**Možete mi dati razmjenu u sitnišu?**
I think you've made a mistake.	**Mislim, da ste napravili grešku.**

10. COMMUNICATIONS

Mail - Pošta

In addition to the regular postal services, the main branch post office provides international telegram and telephone services as well. In Zagreb, the main post office is open 24 hours. Packages to be sent out of Croatia must be brought to a post office unwrapped. Once there, they will be weighed, inspected, wrapped, and stamped.

Letter/Letters - Pismo/Pisma

Where's the nearest post office?	**Gdje je najbliža pošta?**
Where's the main post office?	**Gdje je glavna pošta?**
When does the post office open/close?	**Kad se otvara/ zatvara poštani ured?**
The post office is open from 9 to 6.	**Pošta je otvorena od 9:00 do 18:00.**
Where can I find a mailbox?	**Gdje mogu naći poštansku kutiju?**
Can I buy…here?	**Mogu li ovdje kupit…?**
envelopes	**omotnice**
postcards	**razglednice**
stamps	**poštanske marke**
Please give me ten airmail stamps for letters/postcards to the USA.	**Molim vas dajte mi deset avionskih maraka za pisma/ razglednice za USA.**
I'd like to send this letter/postcard by…	**Htio bi poslati ovo pismo/razglednicu…**

surface mail.	**kopnenom poštom.**
airmail.	**zrakoplovnom poštom.**
registered mail.	**registrirano pimso.**
special delivery.	**preporučeno pismo.**
Will this go out today?	**Dali će ovo biti poslano danas?**
I'd like to send this to…	**Htio bi ovo poslat za…**
America.	**Ameriku.**
Canada.	**Kanadu.**
England.	**Englesku.**
France.	**Francusku.**
Germany.	**Njemačku.**
I'd like to send this parcel.	**Htio bi ovo poslati u paketu.**
It contains books/ souvenirs/fragile material.	**Sadrži knjige/ suvenire/lako lomljive stvari.**
Wrap it up, please.	**Omotajte ovo, molim vas.**
Write the address here.	**Ovdje napišite adresu.**
return address	**povratna adresa**
Have I received any mail?	**Dali sam dobio (m.)/ dobila (f.) ikakvu poštu?**
My name is…	**Moje ime je…**
Here is my passport.	**Evo moj pasoš.**

Telegrams - Telegrams

I'd like to send a telegram.	**Htio (m.)/Htjela (f.) bi poslati telegram.**

COMMUNICATIONS

Where can I send a telegram?	**Odkud mogu poslati telegram?**
May I have an international form?	**Dajte mi, molim vas, međunarodnu formu?**
What is the rate per word?	**Koliko se plati po riječi?**
What will be the total cost?	**Koliko će sveukupno koštati?**
How long will it take to reach the USA?	**Kako dugo će uzeti da to dođe u Ameriku?**

Telephones - Telefoni

Phonebooks exist in Croatia, but they are not available in every hotel room. Local calls can be made at any time from any phone. International calls, however, can only be made at the telephone office of the main post office or through your hotel. They must be booked in advance. To make a local call from a phone booth, you first drop in a coin, pick up the receiver, wait for a long continuous buzz, then dial. Long signals mean the phone is ringing; shorter ones mean the line is busy.

public phone	**gradski telefon**
Where's the nearest telephone?	**Gdje je najbliži telefon?**
May I use your phone?	**Mogu li upotrebit vaš telefon?**
Hello? (on the phone)	**Halo?**
Who is this?	**Tko govori?**
This is...	**Ovo je...**

My name is…	**Moje ime je…**
I'd like to speak to…	**Htio (m.)/Htjela (f.)** **bi govorit sa…**
He/She isn't in.	**On/ona nije ovdje.**
When will he/she return?	**Kad će se on/ona** **vratiti?**
Tell him/her that I called.	**Recite njemu/njoj da** **sam zvao (m.)/** **zvala (f.).**
Take a message, please.	**Molim vas hoćete** **uzet poruku.**
My number is…	**Moj telefonski broj** **je…**
Ask him/her to call me back.	**Pitajte njega/nju da** **me nazove.**
I don't understand.	**Ne razumijem.**
Do you speak English?	**Dali govorite** **Engleski?**
I can't hear you.	**Nečujem vas.**
Can you speak slower/louder?	**Možete li govorit** **sporije/glasnije?**
With whom do you want to speak?	**S kim hoćete da** **govorite?**
You've got the wrong number. Dial again.	**Zvali ste krivi broj,** **zovite ponovo.**
The number has been changed.	**Broj telefona se** **promjenio.**
The phone is broken.	**Telefon je pokvaren.**
international phone call	**međunarodni** **telefonski poziv**
Can I dial direct?	**Mogu li zvati** **direktno?**

Operator, please get me this number.	**Molim vas operator, možete mi nazvat ovaj broj.**
I'd like to place a phone call to the USA.	**Htio bi (m.)/Htjela (f.) bi telefonski poziv za Ameriku.**
How much does a call to New York cost?	**Koliko košta poziv do New York-a?**
What number are you calling?	**Koji broj zovete?**
Do I have long to wait?	**Dali moram dugo čekati?**
How long do you want to speak?	**Koliko vremena hoćete govoriti?**
Wait a minute.	**Pričekajte malo, vaš poziv.**
Your call is in booth number two.	**Je u kabini broj dva.**
How much did the call cost?	**Koliko je poziv koštao?**
There's a call for you.	**Imate telefonski poziv.**
Hold on, please.	**Pričcekajte moment, molim.**
It's busy.	**Telefon je zauzet.**
There's no answer.	**Nitko ne odgovara.**
I can't get through.	**Nemogu dobit kontakt.**
We've been cut off.	**Razgovor nam je prekinut.**

11. SERVICES

Dry Cleaning/Laundry - Čišćenje/Pranje Rublja

Laundry and dry cleaning services are usually available in your hotel. Ask the desk clerk for details and assistance.

Where can I get my laundry washed?	**Gdje mogu oprati moju robu/rublje?**
I need these things…	**Trebam ove stvari…**
dry-cleaned.	**parno čišćenje.**
ironed.	**ispeglati.**
washed.	**oprati.**
No starch, please.	**Bez škroba, molim.**
Can you get this stain out?	**Možete li odstranit ovu mrlju?**
Can you mend/sew this?	**Možete li ovo zaštopat/zašit?**
Sew this button on, please.	**Molim vas prišijte mi ovo dugme.**
When will it be ready?	**Kad će biti gotovo?**
Is my laundry ready?	**Jeli moj veš gotov?**
How much do I owe you?	**Koliko vam dugujem?**
This isn't mine.	**Ovo nije moje.**
I'm missing something.	**Nešto mi nedostaje.**
This is torn.	**Ovo je potrgano.**
Can I borrow a needle and thread?	**Mogu li posuditi iglu i konac?**
scissors	**nožice; škare**

Optician - Liječnik za Oči

Where can I find an optician?	Gdje mogu naći liječnika za oči?
I have broken my glasses.	Slomio(m.)/Slomila (f.) sam naočale.
The frame is broken.	Okvir je slomljen.
The lenses are broken.	Leće su slomljene.
Can you fix them?	Možete ih popraviti?
How long will it take?	Kako dugo će uzeti?
Here's my prescription.	Evo mog recepta.
Can you replace it?	Dali je možete zamjenit?

Shoe Repair - Popravak Obuće

Shine my shoes, please.	Molim vas očistite mi cipele.
Can these shoes be repaired?	Dali ove cipele mogu biti popravljene?
I need new soles/heels.	Trebam novi đon/ pete.
The heel is broken.	Slomila mi se peta.
Can this be sewn up?	Može li ovo biti zašiveno?
How much will it cost?	Koliko će koštati?
When will they be ready?	Kad će biti gotove?

Barber/Hairdresser - Brijač/Frizer

Where is the nearest barber?	Gdje je najbliži brijač?
Is there a hairdresser in the hotel?	Dali ima frizerski salon u hotelu?
Can I make an appointment?	Mogu li napraviti rezervaciju?

Have a seat.	**Sjednite.**
haircut/hairstyle	**ošišat se/uredit frizuru**
part (hair)	**rzdjeliti kosu**
dye	**bojanje kose**
A hair cut, please.	**Šišanje, molim.**
Just a trim.	**Samo podkresat.**
Take a little off the sides, please.	**Poskinite malo sa strane, molim.**
Not too short.	**Ne mnogo kratko.**
Just a little more, please.	**Samo još malo, molim.**
Shampoo and set, please.	**Oprat kosu i namjestit, molim.**
Blow-dry my hair.	**Osušite mi kosu.**
A shave, please.	**Obrijte me, molim.**
Trim my beard/mustache/ sideburns.	**Potkratite moju bradu/brkove/ zaliske.**
Dye my hair this color.	**Obojite mi kosu. u ovoj boji.**
I would like a facial/ manicure.	**Htio bi (m.)/Htjela bi (f.) masažu lica/ manikuru.**
Thank you.	**Hvala.**
How much do I owe?	**Koliko vam dugujem?**

Film Development - Razvijanje Filma

It is best to bring enough film and photography supplies from home for your entire trip. If you do purchase Croatian film, be sure to have it developed at a photo lab before you leave, as Croatian processing procedures differ from ours. It is impolite to photograph people without their permission.

photography	**fotografija**
camera	**fotoparat**
film	**film**
black and white film	**crno-bjeli film**
color film	**film u boji**
36 exposures	**s trideset šest snimaka**
How much does processing cost?	**Koliko košta razvijanje filma?**
I'd like this enlarged.	**Htio (m.)/Htjela (f.) bi ovo povećati.**
I'd like another copy of this print.	**Htio bi još jednu kopiju ove ekspoze.**
When will they be ready?	**Kad će da budu gotove?**

12. TRANSPORTATION

Public transportation in Croatia is inexpensive, clean, and efficient. Buses and streetcars run from 6:00 A.M. to 1:00 A.M. Tickets are usually purchased on board or at the bus stops. Spot checks are done occasionally and passengers without tickets are fined. Stops are well-marked with signs. These signs carry the name of the stop and the terminal stop. All routes are denoted by numbers, which are found on the front of the car or bus.

transportation	**prevoz**
bus	**autobus**
streetcar	**tramvaj**
trolley	**trolejbus**
Where is the bus stop?	**Gdje je stanica autobusa?**
How often does the bus/ streetcar run?	**Kako često prolazi autobus/tramvaj?**
When's the next bus?	**Kad je idući autobus?**
bus driver	**kondukter**
fare	**cjena karte**
monthly pass	**mjesečna karta**
Pass me a ticket, please.	**Dodajte mi kartu, molim.**
What bus do I take to the main station?	**Koji autobus ide za glavni kolodvor?**
Do I have to transfer?	**Dali trebam presjedat ?**
Does this bus go near the Technical University?	**Dali ovaj autobus ide pored Tehničkog Fakulteta?**

How many stops until we reach the center of town?	**Koliko ima stanica do centra grada?**
You're on the wrong bus.	**Na krivom ste autobusu.**
Can you tell me where to get off?	**Možete mi reći gdje da siđem?**
You've missed your stop.	**Promašili ste vašu stanicu.**
Are you getting off?	**Dali silazite?**
I want to get off here/ at the next stop.	**Htio bi sići na ovoj/ na idućoj stanici.**
Excuse me, may I pass?	**Molim, mogu li proćI?**
Excuse me, I'm getting off at the next stop.	**Oprostite, ja silazim na idućoj stanici.**
Wait! I'd like to get off!	**Samo malo! Ja silazim ovdje!**

Taxi - Taksi

In addition to being ordered by phone, taxis can be found in front of major hotels and at taxi stands. It is common to share cabs with strangers.

Where can I get a taxi?	**Gdje mogu dobit taksi?**
Where is the nearest taxi stand?	**Gdje je najbliža taksi stanica?**
Please call me a taxi.	**Molim nazovite mi taksi.**
Are you free?	**Dali ste slobodni?**
Where do you want to go?	**Gdje hoćete ići?**
Here's the address.	**Evo adrese.**
To the opera theater, please.	**Do kazališta, molim.**

How much will the ride cost?	**Koliko će vožnja koštati?**
Can you get my bags, please?	**Možete donijeti moje kofere, molim?**
I'm (not) in a hurry.	**Žuri (ne) žuri mi se.**
Stop here.	**Stanite ovdje.**
Wait for me here.	**Čekajte me ovdje.**
I'll be back in a couple of minutes.	**Vratit ću se za par minuta.**
Keep the change.	**Zadržite kusur.**
Thank you.	**Hvala lijepo.**
Welcome/Goodbye.	**Dobro došli/Zbogom.**

Boats - Čamci/Brodovi

boat/motor boat	**čamac/motorni čamac**
ship	**brod**
tour	**ekskurzija**
When does the next one leave?	**Kad idući odlazi?**
Where do we get tickets?	**Gdje se mogu kupit putne karte?**
How much are the tickets?	**Koliko košta putna karta?**
Where is the pier?	**Gdje je mol?**
How long is the trip?	**Kako dugo traje putovanje?**
Where do we stop?	**Gdje pristajemo?**
deck	**paluba**
cabin	**kabina**
life jacket	**pojas za spašavanje**
lifeboat	**čamac za spašavanje**
I feel seasick.	**Ne osjećam se dobro.**

TRANSPORTATION

Trains - Vlakovi

Like all long-distance travel in Croatia, train trips must be reserved in advance. You can usually make reservations through your hotel.

train	**vlak**
train station	**kolodvor**
ticket office	**šalter za karte**
When does the ticket office open?	**Kad se šalter za prodaju karata otvara?**
information office	**informacije**
express long-distance train	**brzi vlak**
standard long-distance train	**putnički vlak**
local train	**tramvaj**
deluxe class	**medunarodni vagon**
first class	**prva klasa**
second class	**druga klasa**
one-way ticket	**karta u jednom pravcu**
round-trip ticket	**povratna karta**
time table	**vozni red**
departure time	**vrijeme odlaska**
arrival time	**vrijeme dolaska**
When is the next train to Split?	**Kad je idući vlak za Split?**
Is it a direct train?	**Da li ide direktno?**
Do I have to change trains?	**Da li trebam presjedati?**
What's the fare to Karlovac?	**Koliko košta do Karlovca?**

I'd like to reserve a berth in the sleeping car.	**Htio bi rezervirati ležište u spavaćim kolima.**
From what platform does the train to Sisak leave?	**S kojeg perona polazi vlak za Sisak?**
When does the train arrive in Zagreb?	**Kad vlak stiže u Zagreb?**
Are we on time?	**Jeli vlak na vrijeme ?**
The train is twenty minutes late.	**Vlak kasni dvadeset minuta.**
Where are we now?	**Gdje smo sad?**
How long do we stop here?	**Kako dugo stojimo ovdje?**
Is there time to get off?	**Dali je dosta vremena da siđemo s vlaka?**
Is this seat taken?	**Jeli ovo mjesto zauzeto?**
This is my seat.	**Ovo je moje sjedalo.**
Am I bothering you?	**Dali vas smetam?**
Can I open/shut the window?	**Mogu li otvorit/ zatvorit prozor?**
Can I turn out/on the light?	**Mogu li upaliti/ ugasiti svjetlo?**
I'd like the top/ bottom bunk.	**Htio (m.)/Htjela (f.) bi gornji/donji ležaj.**
We'd like some tea.	**Htjeli bi malo čaja.**
Two glasses, please.	**Dvije čaše, molim.**
Where is the...	**Gdje je...**
baggage room?	**odjel za prtljagu?**
bathroom?	**zahod?**
conductor?	**kondukter?**
dining car?	**vagon za ručanje?**
gate?	**izlaz?**

porter?	**nosač?**
platform?	**peron?**
sleeping car?	**spavaća kola/vagon?**
(my) sleeping compartment?	**(moj) spavaći kupej?**
smoking car?	**vagon za pušenje?**
snack bar?	**bufet?**
ticket checker?	**kontrolor?**
waiting room?	**čekaona?**
Have a good trip!	**Sretno putovanje!**

Planes - Zrakoplovi

airport	**aerodrom**
arrival	**dolazak**
departure	**odlazak**
boarding pass	**ulazna karta**
I'd like to make a reservation.	**Htio (m.)/Htjela (f.) bi napraviti rezervaciju.**
I'd like a flight to Dubrovnik.	**Htio bi let za Dubrovnik.**
Is there a direct flight?	**Dali ima direktan let?**
How long is the layover?	**Kako dugo moram tamo čekati?**
When is the next flight?	**Kad je idući let?**
Is there a connection to Hvar?	**Dali ima tamo spoj za Hvar?**
one-way ticket	**kartu u jednom pravcu**
round-trip ticket	**povratnu kartu**
Is flight number 5 on time?	**Jeli let broj pet na vrijeme?**

I'd like to change/confirm my flight.	**Htio (m.)/Htjela (f.) bi promjenit/ potvrdit moj let.**
I'd like to cancel my reservation.	**Htio bi poništiti moju rezervaciju.**
How much luggage am I allowed?	**Koliko kofera mi je dozvoljeno nositi?**
What's the flight number?	**Koji je broj leta?**
What gate do we leave from?	**Odakle uzljećemo?**
boarding gate	**ulaz u zrakoplov**
What time do we leave/arrive?	**U koje vrijeme uzlijećemo/ slijećemo?**
What time should I check in?	**Kad trebam prijavit moje kofere?**
Call the flight attendant.	**Zovite stuardesu.**
Fasten your seat belts.	**Pričvrstite vaš opasač na sjedalu.**
Will food be served?	**Dali će jelo biti servi- rano?**
Can I smoke on board?	**Dali je dozvoljeno pušenje za vrijeme leta?**
Is there a bus from the airport to the city?	**Dali vozi autobus od aerodroma do u grad?**

13. DIRECTIONS

directions	**smjer**
I'm lost.	**Izgubljen (m.)/ Izgubljena (f.) sam.**
Excuse me, can you tell me how to get to… this street? the center of town?	**Oprostite, možete mi reći kako doć do…. ove ulice? u centar grada?**
I'm looking for…	**Tražim…**
Am I going in the right direction?	**Dali idem u pravom smjeru?**
Do you know where…is?	**Dali znate gdje je…?**
Is it far?	**Jeli to daleko?**
Is it close?	**Jeli to blizu?**
Can I walk there?	**Mogu li tamo pješice?**
It would be best to take the bus or a taxi.	**Najbolje bi bilo uzet autobus ili taksi.**
What street is this?	**Koja je ovo ulica?**
Please show me where I am on the map.	**Molim vas pokažite mi na karti gdje sam.**
Go straight ahead.	**Samo idite naprijed.**
Go in this/that direction.	**Idite u ovom/onom pravcu.**
Turn left/right.	**Skrenite lijevo/desno.**
at the next corner	**na idućem raskršću**
at the light	**kod semafora**
Take this road.	**Idite ovim putem.**
You have to go back.	**Trebate se vratit natrag.**

You are on the wrong bus. **Vi ste na krivom autobusu.**

Do I have to transfer? **Dali trebam prelaznu kartu?**

It's there on the right/left. **Tamo je na desno/na lijevo.**

north/south	**sjever/jug**
east/west	**istok/zapad**
after/behind	**poslije/ pozadi**
next to/opposite	**pri/suprotno**
There it is!	**Eno ga!**
this/that way	**ovim/onim putom**
in the north	**na sjeveru**
northward	**sjeverno**
in the south	**na jugu**
southward	**južno**
in the east	**na istoku**
eastward	**istočno**
in the west	**na zapadu**
westward	**zapadno**

14. SIGHTSEEING

Taking a Bus Trip - Putovanje Autobusom

What sights should we see?	**Kakove spomenike budemo vidjeti?**
Where can I sign up for an excursion?	**Gdje mogu da se zapišem za izlet?**
I want to take a bus trip around the city.	**Htio (m.)/Htjela (f.) bi putovat autobusom po gradu.**
I'd like to sign up for this excursion.	**Htio (m.)/Htjela (f.) bi se zapisat za ovaj izlet.**
Do I have to sign up in advance?	**Dali se trebam zapisat unaprijed?**
What does a ticket cost?	**Koliko košta vozna karta?**
When does it leave?	**Kad polazi?**
How long does it last?	**Kako dugo traje?**
When do we get back?	**Kad se vraćamo natrag?**
Will we stop somewhere for lunch?	**Dali se negdje svraćamo za ručak?**
From where does the excursion leave?	**Odakle polazimo na izlet/ekskurziju?**
Is there an English speaking guide?	**Dali vodič govori Engleski?**
Will we have free time there?	**Hoćemo li imati tamo slobodnog vremena?**
When should we be back on the bus?	**Kad se trebamo vratit natrag na autobus?**

Taking a Walking Tour - Izlet Pješke

When does it open/close?	**Kad se otvara/ zatvara?**
I want to sign up for a tour.	**Hoću da se zapišem za izlet.**
When does it start/end?	**Kad izlet počinje/ završava?**
What is the cost?	**Koliko košta?**
Do you sell guidebooks in English?	**Dali prodajete knjigu úputstava na Engleskom?**
Is there a map?	**Imate li zemljovidnu kartu?**
In front of...	**Ispred...**
Behind...	**Pozadi...**
In the middle...	**U sredini...**
On the left of...	**Lijevo od...**
On the right of...	**Desno od...**
Where can I buy postcards?	**Gdje mogu kûpit razglednice?**
How much is the postcard?	**Koliko košta jedna razglednica?**
Can I take pictures?	**Smijem li to slikati?**
I want to see the sights.	**Htio bi vidjeti znamenite spomenike.**
Let's go for a walk.	**Idemo se prošetati.**
What kind of...is that?	**Koja vrsta...je to?**
animal	**životinje**
bird	**ptice**
fish	**ribe**
flower	**cvijeta**
tree	**drveta**

We don't have those at home.	**Mi nemamo tih u našem kraju.**
What a beautiful view!	**O, kakav lijepi pogled!**
What's that building?	**Što je ta zgrada?**
When was it built?	**Kad je sagrađena?**
Who was the architect/artist?	**Tko je bio graditelj/ umjetnik?**
When did he/she live?	**Kad je živio/živila?**
Where's the house where...lived?	**Gdje je kuća u kojoj je...živio?**
Can we go in?	**Smijemo li u nju ući?**
It's very interesting.	**Vrlo je zanimljivo.**
It is...	**To je...**
amazing.	**iznenađujuće.**
beautiful.	**lijepo.**
cute.	**ugodno; drago.**
foreboding.	**nedopustivo.**
great.	**znamenito.**
horrible.	**strašno.**
strange.	**strano.**
terrible.	**grozno.**
ugly.	**ružno; neskladno.**
wonderful.	**zadivljujuće.**
Let's rest.	**Idemo se odmorit.**
I'm tired.	**Ja sam umoran (m.)/ umorna (f.).**
I'm bored.	**Dosadno mi je.**

15. RELIGION

Most places of worship do not mind visitors as long as you observe their customs. It is recommended to dress conservatively. Taking pictures is usually not permitted inside the church.

religion	**vjeroispovjest**
monastery	**samostan**
cathedral	**katedrala**
church	**crkva**
synagogue	**sinagoga**
orthodox church	**istočno-pravoslavna crkva**
saint	**svetac**
altar	**oltar**
incense	**tamjan**
candle	**voštana svijeća**
contribution	**lemozina**
prayers	**molitva**
prayer book	**molitvenik**
rabbi	**rabin**
priest	**svećenik**
cemetery	**groblje**
grave	**grob**
tombstone	**nadgrobni spomenik**
When is the service?	**Kad će se služit misa?**
I would like to look around the church.	**Htio (m.)/Htjela (f.) bi razgledati crkvu.**
May I take a picture?	**Smijem li fotografirat?**

16. SPORTS

sports	**šport**
I enjoy…	**Ja volim/uživam…**
cycling.	**vozit bicikl.**
horseback riding.	**jahanje.**
mountain climbing.	**planinarenje.**
running.	**trčati.**
sailing.	**jedrenje.**
skating.	**sklizanje na ledu.**
skiing.	**skijanje.**
swimming.	**plivanje.**
tennis.	**igrati tenis.**
I want to play tennis.	**Htio bi igrat tenis.**
Can we rent rackets?	**Možemo li unajmit raket za tenis?**
Are there tennis courts here?	**Dali ovdje ima tenis igralište?**
Is there a swimming pool here?	**Dali ima kupaći bazen ovdje?**
Is the water deep?	**Jeli voda duboka?**
Is the water cold?	**Jeli voda hladna?**
No swimming!	**Plivanje zabranjeno!**
I want to lie on the beach.	**Hoću samo ležat na plaži.**
Can I rent…	**Mogu li unajmit…**
a row boat?	**barku sa veslima?**
skates?	**sličuhe?**
skiing equipment?	**pribor za skijanje?**
an umbrella?	**suncobran?**
What's the charge per day?	**Koliko košta na dan?**

Is there a skating rink here?	Dali ovdje ima sala za sklizanje?
Where can I go skiing?	Gdje se mogu skijati?
camping	logorovanje
camping permit	dozvola za logorovanje
camping equipment	pribor za logorovanje
Is swimming allowed?	Dali se smije kupati?
Can we camp here?	Možemo li ovdje raspeti šator?
What's the charge per day/per person?	Koliko se plati na dan/po osobi?
Are there showers/toilets?	Postoje li tuševi/ zahodi?
Where are the toilets?	Gdje su zahodi?
Can we light a fire here?	Smije li se ložit vatra ovdje?
Is there electricity?	Da li ima električne struje?
Can we fish here?	Smijemo li lovit ribu?
Do we need a license?	Trebamo li dozvolu za ribolov?
Can we rent equipment?	Možemo li unajmit pribor?
Where can we get (a)...	Gdje možemo dobit...
can opener?	otvarač za konzerve?
charcoal?	ugalj?
compass?	kompas?
cooking utensils?	pribor za kuhanje?
cooler?	hladnjak?
corkscrew?	vadičep?

firewood?	**drva za vatru?**
first-aid kit?	**paket prve pomoći?**
flashlight?	**lampu s baterijom?**
kerosene?	**petroulja?**
lantern?	**lampu?**
matches?	**šibice?**
sleeping bag?	**vreću za spavanje?**
tent?	**šator?**
thermos?	**termos flašu?**

17. ENTERTAINMENT

Tickets – Ulaznice

entertainment	**zabava**
Can you recommend a(n) opera/concert/play?	**Možete li preporučit koju operu/ koncert/igru da vidim?**
Do you have any tickets for tonight's performance?	**Imate li ulaznica za večerašnju predstavu?**
How much are they?	**Koliko koštaju?**
I'd like two for...	**Htio bi dvije za...**
We're sold out.	**Sve je rasprodano.**
What time does it begin?	**U koje vrijeme predstava počinje?**
How do I get to this theater?	**Kako mogu doći do kazališta?**
No admittance after the third bell.	**Nema ulaza po početku predstave.**

amphitheater	**glavna dvorana**
balcony	**balkon**
box	**loža**
coatroom	**garderoba**
lobby	**foaje/hodnik**
orchestra stalls	**parter-lože**
smoking room	**odio za pušenje**
snack bar	**bufet**

entrance to auditorium	**ulaz u auditorium**
exit	**izlaz**
left side	**ljeva strana**

| right side | **desna strana** |
| middle | **sredina** |

Movies - Kino

What's playing at the...	**što se prikazuje u...**
What kind of movie is it?	**Koja vrsta filma je?**
It is a...	**To je...**
action movie.	**divlji zapad/ gangsteri.**
comedy.	**zabavni film.**
documentary.	**dokumentarni film.**
drama.	**drama.**
Who's the director?	**Tko je režiser?**
Who's starring?	**Tko igra glavnu ulogu?**
Are there any tickets left?	**Dali još ima ulaznica?**
Is there a matinee?	**Ima li rana predstava/ matine?**
When does the movie begin?	**Kad predstava počinje?**
Do you have extra tickets?	**Imate li jedan tiket viška?**

Opera, Concerts, & Ballet - Opera, Koncert, & Balet

orchestra	**orkestar**
folk songs/dances	**narodne pjesme/ plesovi**
Here is my ticket.	**Evo moje ulaznice.**
Where is my seat?	**Gdje je moje sjedalo?**
Follow me.	**Slijedite me.**

How much for a program?	**Koliko košta program?**
May I have a program, please?	**Mogu li dobit program, molim?**
Would you like to rent opera glasses?	**Dali hoćete iznajmit operski dalekozor?**
No, thank you.	**Hvala, ne.**
I don't need them.	**Nije mi potreban.**
Who is the conductor?	**Tko je dirigent?**
Who is dancing the lead?	**Tko pleše u glavnoj ulozi?**
Who is the soloist?	**Tko je solista?**
When is the intermission?	**Kad je pauza?**
How long is the intermission?	**Kako dugo traje pauza?**
Pardon me, may I pass?	**Oprostite, mogu li da prođem?**
That's my seat.	**To je moje sjedalo.**

Sporting Events - Športska Natjecanja

sports fan	**športski navijači**
scoreboard	**tabla za rezultat**
I would like to see a soccer game.	**Htio bi vidjet nogometnu utakmicu.**
How much are tickets?	**Koliko košta ulaznica?**
Are there any tickets for today's game?	**Dali ima ulaznica za današnju utakmicu?**
How do I get to Central Stadium?	**Kako da dođem do glavnog stadiona?**
Who is playing?	**Tko igra?**

ENTERTAINMENT

Who is winning?	**Tko vodi/pobjeđuje?**
What's the score?	**Koliki je rezultat?**
It's scoreless.	**Igraju nerješeno.**
Score a goal?	**Dali gol?**
Who won?	**Tko je pobjedio?**
Scoreless tie.	**Bez gola, nerješeno.**
Do you want to play chess?	**Hoćete li igrat šah?**

18. SHOPPING

Stores - Prodavaone
Large department stores are usually open from
9:00 A.M. to 8:00 P.M. Food stores typically open at
8:00 A.M. and close at 7:00 P.M. Other shops, like
bookstores and souvenir shops, are open from
10:00 A.M. to 7:00 P.M. Most stores, except those
selling food, are closed on Sundays.

shopping	**kupovanje**
Where can I buy...	**Gdje mogu kupit...**
Where can I find...	**Gdje mogu naći...**
Is there a...near here?	**Jeli tu...blizu?**
antique store	**starinarnica**
bakery	**pekarna**
bookstore/library	**knjižara/biblioteka**
candy store	**slastičarna**
clothing store	**prodavaona odjeće**
dairy	**Mljekara**
department store	**robna kuća**
drugstore	**ljekarna; apoteka**
farmers market	**tržnica**
fruit/vegetable store	**prodavaona voća/ povrča**
furrier	**krznarija**
gift shop	**rodavaona suvenira**
grocery	**dućan za namirnice**
hat shop	**prodavaona šešira**
jeweler	**zlatarija**
liquor store	**prodavaona pića**
newsstand	**trafika**

record store	**prodavaona kaseta**
shoe store	**prodavaona obuće**
tobacco shop	**prodaja cigareta**
toy store	**dućan za igračke**

Browsing - Razgledanje

Can you help me?	**Možte mi pomoći?**
Where's the department?	**Gdje je odjeljenje?**
Can I help you?	**Mogu li vam pomoći?**
Do you have…	**Dali imate…**
What kind would you like?	**Kakvu vrstu bi vi htjeli?**
I'd like….	**Htio (m.)/Htjela (f.) bi…**
I'm sorry, we don't have any.	**Žao mi je, ali nemamo ništa.**
We're sold out.	**Sve je rasprodano.**
Anything else?	**Nešto drugo?**
Could you please show me this/that?	**Pokažite mi ovo/ono molim?**
No, not that, but the other one next to it.	**Ne, ne to, nego naredno do toga.**
It's not what I want.	**To nije što ja hoću.**
I don't like it.	**To mi se ne sviđa.**
I'm just looking.	**Samo razgledam.**
I prefer…	**Ja bi rađe…**
Something not too expensive.	**Nešto ne mnogo skupo.**
How much is it?	**Koliko ovo košta?**
Please repeat that.	**Ponovite to molim.**
Please write it down.	**Molim vas napišite to.**

Making A Purchase - Kako Kupovati

Have you decided?	**Dali ste se odlučili?**
Yes, I want this.	**Da, ja hoću ovo.**
I'll take it.	**Uzet ću to.**
Will I have problems with customs?	**Dali ću imat problema s carinom?**
Pay at the cashier.	**Platite na blagajni.**
Do you accept traveler's checks/credit cards?	**Mogu li platiti travelers čekom/ kreditnom kartom?**
May I have a receipt?	**Mogu li dobit potvrdu?**
Please wrap it up for me.	**Zamotajte mi to molim.**
May I please have a bag?	**Molim vas dajte mi škanicl?**

Gifts & Souvenirs - Pokloni & Suveniri

books	**knjige**
box of candy	**kutija bonbona**
chocolate	**čokolada**
cigarettes	**cigarete**
cigarette lighter	**pripaljivač**
coins	**stari novac/ numezmatika**
fur hat	**krzneni šešir**
jewelry	**nakiti**
lace	**čipke**
perfume	**mirisi; parfemi**
plum brandy	**šljivovica**
postcards	**razglednice**
posters	**oglasi**

SHOPPING

records	**gramofonske ploče**
stamps	**poštanske marke**
tapes	**kasete**
toys	**igračke**
wine	**vino**
wood carvings	**drvo rezbarija**

Jewelry Department - Zlatarija

bracelet	**narukvica**
brooch	**broš**
chain	**lančić**
clips	**spone**
earrings	**naušnice**
necklace	**ogrlica**
ring	**prsten**
tie pin	**spona za kravatu**
watch	**ručni sat**

Stones & Metals - Kamen & Metali

What is this made of?	**Od čega je to napravljeno?**
Is it real gold/silver?	**Da li je zlato/srebro?**
How many carats is it?	**Koliko karata to ima?**
What kind of metal/ stone is it?	**Koja vrsta metala/ kamena je to?**
amber	**jantar**
amethyst	**amatist**
copper	**bakar**
coral	**koralj**
crystal	**kristal**
diamond	**dijamant**
ebony	**ebonovina**

emerald	**smaragd**
garnet	**granat**
gilded	**pozlaćeno**
glass	**staklo**
gold	**zlato**
ivory	**slonova kost**
onyx	**oniks**
pearl	**biser**
pewter	**kositar**
platinum	**platina**
ruby	**rubin**
sapphire	**safir**
silver	**srebro**
silver-plated	**posrebreno**

**Books & Stationery Supplies -
Knjige & Pisaći Pribor**

bookstore	**knjižara**
newsstand	**trafika; novine**
second-hand bookstore	**rabljene knjige; antikvarijat**
stationery store	**papirnica**
Do you have any books in English?	**Dali imate neku knjigu na Engleskom?**
Do you have any children's books?	**Dali imate knjiga za djecu?**
Where are the guidebooks/dictionaries?	**Gdje su kmjige za vodiče/rječnici ?**
Where do I pay?	**Gdje da platim?**
How much is this book?	**Koliko košta ova knjiga?**

Do you have any…	Imate li ijedan…
calendars?	klendar?
envelopes?	omotnice?
magazines in English?	časopise na engleskom?
maps?	zemljovidne karte?
notebooks?	notese?
paper?	papir?
pens?	kemijske olovke?
pencils?	olovke?
postcards?	dopisnice?

Records - Gramofonske Ploče

Do you have a recording by…	Dali imate ijednu gramofonsku ploču od…
Do you have any Croatian folk songs?	Imate li koju Hrvatsku narodnu pjesmu?
Do you have any…	Imate li išta da…
poets reading their work?	pjesnik čita svoje pjesme?
classical music?	klasičnu muziku?
popular music?	popularnu muziku?
recordings of operas or plays?	ploče od opera ili kazališnih predstava?
Can I listen to this record?	Mogu li da slušam ovu ploču/kasetu?

Toys/Games - Igračke/Igre

for a boy	za dječaka
for a girl	za djevojčicu

ball	**lopta**
blocks	**kocke**
cards	**karte**
chess	**šah**
doll	**lutke**
electronic game	**elektronske igre**
teddy bear	**medo**
wooden toys	**drvene igračke**

Clothes - Odjeća

Where can I find a...	**Gdje mogu naći...**
bathing cap?	**kapu za kupanje?**
bathing suit?	**kupaći kostim?**
belt?	**remen/kajiš?**
blouse?	**bluzu?**
bra?	**grudnjak?**
children's clothes?	**dječju odjeću?**
coat?	**kaput (dugi)?**
dress?	**haljinu?**
fur coat?	**krzneni kaput?**
fur hat?	**šešir od krzna/ šubaru?**
gloves?	**rukavice?**
handkerchief?	**džepni rupčić?**
hat?	**šešir?**
jacket?	**kaput?**
panties?	**ženske gaćice?**
pants?	**hlače?**
pajamas?	**pidžamu?**
raincoat?	**kišni ogrtač?**
scarf?	**šal?**
shirt?	**košulja?**
shorts?	**kratke hlače?**

skirt?	suknja?
slip?	kombine?
socks?	čarape?
stockings?	ženske čarape?
suit?	odjelo?

Fit - Probe/Mjere

I don't know my size.	Ja neznam moj broj.
I take a size...	Paše mi broj...
Is there a mirror?	Ima li tu ogledalo?
Can I try it on?	Mogu li obući za probu?
Where is the fitting room?	Gdje je kabina za probu?
Does it fit?	Dali mi paše?
It fits well.	Paše vam vrlo dobro.
It doesn't suit me.	Ne pristaje mi.
It's too...	Vrlo mi je...
big/small.	veliko/malo.
long/short.	dugo/kratko.
loose/tight.	široko/tjesno.

Colors - Boje

What color is it?	Koja boja je to?
I don't like the color.	Nevolim ovu boju.
Do you have other colors?	Imate li drugih boja?
I'd like something bright.	Ja bi volio (m.)/volila (f.) nešto svjetlije.
Do you have anything in red?	Imate li išta u crvenom?
black	crno
blue	plavo
brown	smeđe

green	**zeleno**
grey	**sivo**
light blue	**svjetlo-plavo**
orange	**narančasto**
pink	**ružičasto**
red	**crveno**
white	**bjelo**
yellow	**žuto**

light (+color)	**svjetlo (boja)**
dark (+color)	**tamno (boja)**

Materials & Fabrics - Materijali & Tkanine

aluminum	**aluminij**
brass	**bronza**
canvas	**platno**
ceramics	**keramika**
chiffon	**šifon**
china	**porcelan**
copper	**bakar**
cotton	**pamuk**
crystal	**kristal**
fabric	**tkanina**
felt	**felt**
flannel	**flanel**
fur	**krzno**
glass	**staklo**
gold	**zlato**
iron	**željezo**
lace	**čipka**
leather	**koža**
linen	**platno**
metal	**metal**

nylon	**najlon**
plastic	**plastika**
satin	**saten**
silk	**svila**
silver	**srebro**
steel	**čelik**
stone	**kamen**
velvet	**velvet**
wood	**drvo**
wool	**vuna**

Shoes - Cipele

shoe store	**prodavaona obuće**
boots	**čizme**
sandals	**sandale**
slippers	**papuče**
children's shoes	**dječije cipele**
shoelaces	**privezice**
Are these made of cloth/leather/rubber?	**Dali je ovo načinjeno od platna/kože/ gume?**
Can I try these on in a size…	**Mogu li probati ove u broju…**
These are too big/small/ narrow/wide.	**Ove su vrlo velike/ male/uske/široke.**

Groceries - Namirnice

grocery store	**prodavaona namirnica**
I'd like…	**Ja bi htio (m.)/ htjela (f.)…**
a piece of that.	**dio toga.**
a half kilo.	**pola kila.**

one and a half kilos.	**kilo i pol.**
50 grams.	**50 grama.**
100 grams.	**100 grama.**
a liter of...	**jedan litar...**
a bottle of...	**jednu flašu...**
ten eggs.	**deset jaja.**
a packet of cookies/tea.	**kutiju keksa/čaja.**
a can of pears.	**konzervu krušaka.**
a loaf of bread.	**štrucu kruha.**
a box of candy.	**kutiju bonbona.**
a bar of chocolate.	**komad čokolade.**

Health & Beauty Aids - Stvari Za Zdravlje i Ljepotu

absorbent cotton	**vata**
antiseptic	**antiseptik**
aspirin	**aspirin**
ace bandage	**elastični omotač**
bobby pins	**spone**
comb	**češalj**
condoms/contraceptives	**prezervativ**
cough drops	**tablete za kašalj**
disinfectant	**dezifektant**
eardrops	**kâpi za uho**
eyedrops	**kâpi za oči**
hairbrush	**četku za kosu**
hair dye	**tintu za bojanje kose**
hair spray	**lak za kosu**
hand cream	**kremu za ruke**
iodine	**jod**
lipstick	**ruž**
make-up	**šminku**
nail clipper	**nožice za nokte**

nail file	**turpiju za nokte**
nail polish	**lak za nokte**
nail polish remover	**aceton**
pacifier	**dudla**
perfume	**parfem**
razor	**britva**
razor blades	**žileti**
safety pins	**zapinjače**
sanitary napkins	**sanitarni ulošci**
shampoo	**šampon**
shaving cream	**krema za brijanje**
sleeping pills	**tablete za spavanje**
soap	**sapun**
suntan lotion	**ulje za sunčanje**
thermometer	**toplomjer**
toilet paper	**toaletni papir**
toothbrush	**četka za zube**
toothpaste	**pasta za zube**
tweezers	**pinceta**
vitamins	**vitamini**

19. HEALTHCARE

Seeing a Doctor - Doktorska Posjeta

healthcare	**zdravstvena briga**
I'd like an appointment...	**Htio bi rezervirat posjetu...**
for tomorrow.	**za sutra.**
as soon as possible.	**što je moguće prije.**
Where does it hurt?	**Gdje te boli?**
Is the pain sharp/ dull/constant?	**Dali je bol oštar/blag/ dugotrajan?**
How long have you felt this way?	**Kako dugo se ovako osjećate?**
I'll take your temperature.	**Izmjerit ću vam temperaturu.**
I'll measure your blood pressure.	**Izmjerit ću vam krvni tlak.**
I'll take your pulse.	**Izmjerit ću vam bilo.**
Roll up your sleeve.	**Zavrnite rukav.**
Undress to the waist.	**Svucite se do pasa.**
Breathe deeply.	**Dišite duboko.**
Open your mouth.	**Otvorite usta.**
Cough.	**Kašljite.**
I'll need an x-ray.	**Trebat ću rengensku sliku.**
Is it serious?	**Dali je opasna stvar?**
Do I need surgery?	**Dali trebam operaciju?**
It's broken/sprained.	**slomljen je/ uganjen.**
You need a cast.	**Potreban vam je gips.**
You've pulled a muscle.	**Istegnuli ste mišić.**

It's infected.	**Imate upalu.**
It's not contagious.	**Nije prelazno.**
Get well.	**Ubrzo ozdravite.**

Seeing a Dentist - Posjet Zubaru

I need a dentist.	**Trebam zubara.**
What are the clinic's hours?	**Kakav je raspored kliničke posjete?**
I want to make an appointment.	**Hoću rezervirat posjetu k doktoru.**
Will I have to wait long?	**Trebam li dugo čekati?**
I have...	**Imam...**
an abscess.	**upalu desni.**
a broken tooth.	**slomljen zub.**
a broken denture.	**slomljenu zubnu protezu.**
lost a filling.	**ispala mi je plomba.**
a toothache.	**boli me zub.**
a cavity.	**izoban zub.**
sore and bleeding gums.	**bole me i krvare desni.**
Don't pull it out.	**Nemojte ga izvaditi.**
Can you fix it temporarily?	**Možete li ga popraviti privremeno?**
When will my denture be ready?	**Kad će moja proteza biti gotova?**
May I have an anesthetic?	**Mogu li dobit nešto za ublaženje bolova?**

Treatment - Liječenje

I'm taking medication.	**Trošim ljekove.**
What medicine are you taking?	**Koje ljekove trošite?**
I'm taking antibiotics.	**Uzimljem antibiotike.**
I'm on the Pill.	**Trošim tablete protiv trudnoće.**
I'm allergic to penicillin.	**Ja sam alergičan na penicilin.**
I'll prescribe an...	**Propisat ću vam...**
antibiotic.	**antibiotik.**
a painkiller.	**lijek za ublaženje bolova.**
Where can I have this prescription filled?	**Gdje mogu ove lijekove dobiti?**
When should I take the medicine?	**Kad trebam uzeti lijekove?**
Take 2 pills/3 teaspoons...	**Uzmite 2 tablete/ 3 žličice...**
every 2/6 hours.	**svaka 2/6 sati.**
twice a day.	**dvaput dnevno.**
before meals.	**prije jela.**
after meals.	**poslije jela.**
as needed.	**po potrebi.**
for 5/10 days.	**za 5/10 dana.**
I feel better/worse/ the same.	**Osjećam se bolje/ lošije/jednako.**
Can I travel on Friday?	**Mogu li putovati u ovaj petak?**

At the Hospital - U Bolnici

hospital	**bolnica**
clinic	**ambulanta**

doctor	**doktor/liječnik**
surgeon	**kirurg**
gynecologist	**doktor za ženske bolesti**
ophthalmologist	**doktor za oči**
pediatrician	**dječiji liječnik**
nurse	**bolničar/bolničarka**
patient	**bolesnik/pacijent**
bedpan	**noćna posuda**
injection	**inekcija**
operation	**operacija**
transfusion	**transfuzija krvi**
thermometer	**toplomjer/ termometar**
I can't sleep/eat.	**Nemogu spavati/jesti.**
When will the doctor come?	**Kad će doktor da dođe?**
When can I get out of bed?	**Kad ću se moći dići iz kreveta?**
When are visiting hours?	**Kad je vrijeme posjete?**

Parts of the Body - Djelovi Tjela

ankle	**gležanj**
appendix	**slijepo crijevo**
arm	**ruka**
back	**leđa**
bladder	**mokraćni mjehur**
blood	**krv**
body	**tjelo**
bone	**kost**
breasts	**dojke**
calf	**list**

cheek	**jagodica**
chest cavity	**grudni koš**
ear/ears	**uho/uši**
elbow	**lakat**
eye	**oko/oči (pl.)**
face	**obraz**
finger	**prst**
foot	**stopalo**
gall bladder	**žuč**
genitalia	**spolni organi**
glands	**žljezde**
hand	**podlaktica**
heart	**srce**
heel	**peta**
hip	**bok**
intestines	**crijeva**
jaw	**vilica**
joint	**zglob**
kidney	**bubreg**
knee	**koljeno**
leg	**noga**
lip	**usna**
liver	**jetra**
lungs	**pluća**
mouth	**usta**
muscle	**mišić**
neck	**vrat**
nerve	**živac**
nose	**nos**
rib	**rebro**
shoulder	**rame**
skin	**koža**
spine	**kičma**

stomach	**želudac**
teeth	**zubi**
tendon	**tetiva**
throat	**grlo**
thumb	**palac**
toe	**nožni palac**
tongue	**jezik**
tonsils	**krajnici**
vein	**vena; krvna žila**
wrist	**ručni zglob**

20. EMERGENCY

emergency	**hitna pomoć**
I need help.	**Trebam pómôć.**
There's been an accident.	**Desila se nesreća.**
Please call the…	**Molim vas pozovite…**
ambulance.	**hitnu pomoć.**
American embassy.	**Američku ambasadu.**
British embassy.	**Englesku ambasadu.**
Consulate.	**Konzulat.**
Please get…	**Molim vas pozovite…**
a doctor.	**doktora.**
the police.	**policiju.**
Please notify…	**Molim vas obavjestite…**
my husband.	**mog supruga/muža.**
my wife.	**moju suprugu/ženu.**
my family.	**moju obitelj.**
my hotel.	**moj hotel.**
I've had my….stolen.	**Netko mi je ukrao…**
I've lost my…	**Izgubio (m.)/Izgubila (f.) sam moj…**
passport.	**pasoš.**
wallet.	**novčanik.**
purse.	**tašku.**
keys.	**ključeve.**
money.	**novac.**

Illness and Injury - Bolesti i Ozljede

He/She is hurt.	**On/Ona je ozlijeđen/a (m./f.).**
He/She is bleeding badly.	**On/Ona mnogo krvari.**

He/She is unconscious.	**On/Ona je u nesvjesti.**
He/She is seriously injured.	**On/ona je teško ozlijeđen/a (m./f.).**
I'm in pain.	**Imam bolove.**
My...hurts.	**Boli me...**
I can't move my...	**Nemogu micati moju...**
I'm ill.	**Ja sam bolestan (m.)/bolesna (f.).**
I'm dizzy.	**Imam vrtoglavicu.**
I'm nauseous.	**Imam mučninu u stomku.**
I feel feverish.	**Imam temperaturu.**
I've vomited.	**Povratio (m.)/ Povratila (f.) sam.**
I've got food poisoning.	**Imam otrovanje hranom.**
I've got diarrhea.	**Imam proljev.**
It hurts to swallow.	**Boli me kad gutam.**
I'm having trouble breathing.	**Imam teškoću disati.**
I have chest pain.	**Imam bol u prsima.**
I've got indigestion.	**Boli me stomak.**
I've got a bloody nose.	**Moj nos krvari.**
I've got sunstroke.	**Imam sunčanicu.**
I'm sun-burned.	**Imam sunčane opekotine.**
I've got cramps.	**Imam grčeve.**
I've got a bladder/ vaginal infection.	**Imam upalu mjehura/vaginalnu infekciju.**

I've broken my arm.   **Slomio (m.)/Slomila (f.) sam ruku.**

I've sprained my ankle.   **Uganio (m.)/Uganila (f.) sam gležanj.**

I've dislocated my shoulder.   **Iščašio (m.)/Iščašila (f.) sam rame.**

I've been stung by a wasp/bee.   **Ujela me osa/pčela.**

I've got...   **Ja imam...**
  arthritis.   **reumu.**
  asthma.   **astmu.**
  diabetes.   **šećernu bolest.**
  high blood pressure.   **visok tlak krvi.**
  an ulcer.   **čir na stomku.**

21. NUMBERS

Cardinal Numbers - Glavni brojevi

Croatian numbers are highly irregular. The number **one** agrees in gender with the noun it modifies. This means it can be masculine, feminine, or neuter. The number **two** has two forms: one form is both masculine and neuter, the other is strictly feminine. All the remaining numbers have one form for masculine and feminine. The neuter form (for 5-20) is created by adding the suffix (*-ero*).

0	**nula**
1	**jedan/jedna/jedno** (m./f./nt.)
2	**dva/dvije/dvoje** (m./f./nt.)
3	**tri/tri/troje** (m./f./nt.)
4	**četiri/četiri/četvero** (m./f./nt.)
5	**pet-ero** (m. + f./nt.)
6	**šest-ero** (m. + f./nt.)
7	**sedam**
8	**osam**
9	**devet**
10	**deset**
11	**jedanaest**
12	**dvanaest**
13	**trinaest**
14	**četrnaest**
15	**petnaest**
16	**šesnaest**
17	**sedamnaest**
18	**osamnaest**
19	**devetnaest**
20	**dvadeset**

21	**dvadeset jedan**
22	**dvadeset dva**
23	**dvadeset tri**
24	**dvadeset četiri**
25	**dvadeset pet**
26	**dvadeset šest**
27	**dvadeset sedam**
28	**dvadeset osam**
29	**dvadeset devet**
30	**trideset**
31	**trideset jedan**
32	**trideset dva**
33	**trideset tri**
34	**trideset četiri**
35	**trideset pet**
36	**trideset šest**
37	**trideset sedam**
38	**trideset osam**
39	**trideset devet**
40	**četrdeset**
41	**četrdeset jedan**
50	**pedeset**
60	**šezdeset**
70	**sedamdeset**
80	**osamdeset**
90	**devedeset**
100	**sto/stotina**
200	**dvjesta**
300	**trista**
400	**četiri stotine**
500	**petsto**
600	**šeststo**
700	**sedamsto**

800	**osamsto**
900	**devetsto**
1000 ·	**tisuća**
2000	**dvije tisuće**
5000	**pet tisuća**
100,000	**sto tisuća**
1,000,000	**milijun**

Ordinal Numbers - Redovni Brojevi

Since they act as adjectives grammatically, all ordinal numbers have masculine (-*i*), feminine (-*a*), and neuter (-*o*) forms which can be identified by their endings.

first	**prvi/prva/prvo** (m./f./nt.)
second	**drugi/druga/drugo** (m./f./nt.)
third	**treći**
fourth	**četvrti**
fifth	**peti**
sixth	**šesti**
seventh	**sedmi**
eighth	**osmi**
ninth	**deveti**
tenth	**deseti**
eleventh	**jedanaesti**
twelfth	**dvanaesti**
thirteenth	**trinaesti**
fourteenth	**četrnaesti**
fifteenth	**petnaesti**
sixteenth	**šesnaesti**
seventeenth	**sedamnaesti**
eighteenth	**osamnaesti**
nineteenth	**devetnaesti**

twentieth	**dvadeseti**
thirtieth	**trideseti**
fortieth	**četrdeseti**
hundredth	**stoti**
thousandth	**tisući**

22. QUANTITIES & MEASUREMENTS

quantity	**količina**
measurement	**mjere**
a lot/much	**mnogo/mnogo više**
a little/few	**malo/vrlo malo**
more/less	**više/manje**
most/least/best/worst of all	**najviše/najmanje/ najbolje/najgore**
majority/minority	**većina/manjina**
enough/too much	**dosta/previše**
a third	**trećina**
a quarter	**četvrtina**
a half	**polovica**
three quarters	**tri četvrtine**
the whole	**sve**
once	**jednom**
twice	**dvaput**
three times	**triput**
five times	**pet puta**

23. TIME

Days and Weeks - Dani i Tjedni

Monday	**ponedjeljak**
Tuesday	**utorak**
Wednesday	**srijeda**
Thursday	**četvrtak**
Friday	**petak**
Saturday	**subota**
Sunday	**nedjelja**

on Wednesday	**u srijedu**
on Monday	**u ponedjeljak**
last Saturday	**prošle subote**
next Thursday	**idući četvrtak**
from Monday to Friday	**od ponedjeljka do petka**
What day is today?	**Koji dan je danas?**
It's Tuesday.	**Danas je utorak.**
week	**tjedan**
last week	**prošli tjedan**
this week	**ovaj tjedan**
next week	**idući tjedan**
in two weeks	**za dva tjedna**
in five weeks	**za pet tjedana**
every week	**svakog tjedna**
for three weeks	**u toku tri tjedna**
two weeks ago	**pred dva tjedna**

Months - Mjeseci

January	**Sječanj**
February	**Veljača**
March	**Ožujak**

April	**Travanj**
May	**Svibanj**
June	**Lipanj**
July	**Srpanj**
August	**Kolovoz**
September	**Rujan**
October	**Listopad**
November	**Studeni**
December	**Prosinac**

this month	**ovog mjeseca**
last/next month	**prošli/idući mjesec**
every month	**svakog mjeseca**
in a month	**u roku mjesec dana**
We'll be here from June to August.	**Bit ćemo ovdje od lipnja do kolovoza.**
We'll be here from the 3rd of May to July 19th.	**Bit ćemo ovdje od trećeg svibnja do devetnaestog srpnja.**
I've been here since October 14th.	**Ovdje sam još od četrnaestog listopada.**
What's the date?	**Koji je datum?**
It's January 22nd.	**Ovo je dvadeset drugi sječnja.**
When did he arrive?	**Kad je on došao?**
He arrived on May 2nd.	**Doputovao je drugog svibnja.**

Years - Godine

| decade | **desetljeće** |
| century | **stoljeće** |

this year	**ove godine**
next year	**iduće godine**
last year	**prošle godine**
in a year	**u toku godine**
for a year	**za godinu dana**
three years ago	**natrag tri godine**
year-round	**kroz cjelu godinu**
In the 19th century...	**U devetnaestom stoljeću...**
In the 20th century...	**U dvadesetom stoljeću...**
In the 21st century...	**U dvadeset prvom stoljeću...**
In 2010...	**U dvije tisuće i desetoj godini...**
In 1990...	**U tisuću devetsto devedesetoj godini...**
In 1983...	**Tisuću devetsto osamdeset treće...**
How old are you?	**Koliko ste star (m.)/ stara (f.)?**
I'm 28 years old.	**Star (m.)/Stara (f.) sam 28 godina.**
When was he/she born?	**Kad je on/ona rođen (m.)/rođena (f.)?**

Seasons - Godišnja Doba

spring/in the spring	**proljeće/u proljeće**
summer/in the summer	**ljeto/u ljetu**
fall/in the fall	**jesen/u jesen**
winter/in the winter	**zima/u zimi**

Telling Time - Kako Reći Vrijeme

Zagreb, Croatia is six hours ahead of Eastern Standard time and has no Daylight Savings time. Official time is in military format.

time	**vrijeme**
hour	**jedan sat**
half hour	**pola sata**
minute	**minuta**
second	**sekunda**
early/late	**rano/kasno**
now	**sád**
never	**nikad**
still	**još**
sometimes	**ponekad**
usually	**uobičajeno**
often	**često**
always	**stalno/vazda**
in the past	**u prošlosti**
in the future	**u budućnosti**
a long time ago	**davno**
a short time ago	**nédavno**
I'm sorry I'm late.	**Oprostite mi, što sam zakasnio (m.)/ zakasnila (f.).**
on time	**na vrijeme**
What time is it?	**Koliko je sati?**
It's...	**Sad je...**
one o'clock.	**jedan sat.**
five past three.	**tri i pet.**
ten past six.	**šest i deset.**
quarter after four.	**četvrt poslije četiri.**
twenty past twelve.	**dvanaest i dvadeset.**

twenty-five after two.	**dva i dvadeset pet.**
seven thirty.	**sedam i pol.**
quarter to one.	**četvrt do jedan.**
ten of eight.	**deset do osam.**
five of two.	**pet do dva.**
twelve o'clock.	**dvanaest sati.**
midnight	**Ponoć**
noon	**Podne**
morning/A.M.	**ujutro**
afternoon/P.M.	**popodne**
At what time?	**U koje vrijeme?**
At one.	**U jedan sat.**
At 3:05.	**U tri sata i pet minuta.**
At 2:10.	**U dva sata i deset.**
At 5:30.	**U pet i trideset.**
At 7:40.	**U sedam i četrdeset.**

Expressions of Time - Vremenski Izrazi

day	**dan**
night	**noć**
today	**danas**
tomorrow	**sutra**
yesterday	**juče**
day after tomorrow	**prekosutra**
day before yesterday	**prekjuče**
the next day	**idući dan**
three/five days ago	**tri/pet dana unatrag**
morning	**jutro**
in the morning	**ujutro**
this morning	**jutros**
yesterday morning	**jučer ujutro**
tomorrow morning	**sutra ujutro**
all morning	**cjelo jutro**

every morning	**svako jutro**
in the afternoon	**popodne**
this afternoon	**ovo popodne**
yesterday afternoon	**jučer popodne**
tomorrow afternoon	**sutra popodne**
all day	**cio dan**
everyday	**svaki dan**
evening	**večer**
in the evening	**uvečer**
this evening	**večeras**
yesterday evening	**jučer uvečer**
tomorrow evening	**sutra uvečer**
all evening	**cjelo veče**
every evening	**svako veče**
at night	**u noći**
all night	**cjelu noć**
every night	**svaku noć**
holiday	**praznik/svetkovina**
vacation	**godišnji odmor**
school holiday	**skolški praznik**
birthday/name day	**rođendan/imendan**

24. WEATHER

weather	**vrijeme**
What is it like outside?	**Kako je vani?**
What is it usually like here?	**Kakvo je vrijeme obično ovdje?**
What's the forecast for tomorrow?	**Kakova je prognoza za sutra?**
Tomorrow it will rain.	**Sutra će padat kiša.**
Today it's...	**Danas je...**
sunny.	**sunčano.**
overcast.	**oblačno.**
cool.	**hladno.**
warm.	**toplo.**
hot.	**vruće.**
cold.	**studeno.**
humid.	**vlažno.**
foggy.	**maglovito.**
windy.	**puše vjetar.**
What a beautiful day!	**O! Kakav lijepi dan!**
What awful weather!	**Kakvo ružno vrijeme!**
It's raining/snowing.	**Pada kšsa/snijeg.**

25. SIGNS

Signs - Znaci/Oznake

Attention!	**Pozor!**
Careful!	**Oprezno!**
Closed for lunch/ repairs/cleaning.	**Zatvoreno za ručak/radi popravka/čišćcenja.**
Danger!	**Opasnost!**
Don't touch!	**Ne dirati!**
Elevator	**Lift/Električno dizalo**
Emergency exit	**Izlaz u nuždi**
Employee entrance	**Ulaz za službenike**
Entrance	**Ulaz**
Exit	**Izlaz**
Go!	**Idi!**
Information	**Obavjesti/ Informacije**
Keep to the left/right.	**Drži lijevo/desno.**
No admittance!	**Nema primanja!**
No entry!	**Ulaz zabranjen!**
No exit!	**Nema prolaza!**
Stairs	**Stube**
Stop!	**Stani!**
No smoking!	**Zabranjeno pušenje!**
Occupied	**Zauzeto**
Police!	**Policija!**
Prohibited!	**Zabranjeno!**
Push/Pull	**Upri/Povuci**
Quiet!	**Tiho!**
Restrooms	**Zahod muški (m.)/ ženski (f.)**
Self-serve	**Samoposluga**

Up/Down	**Góré/Dolje**
Wait!	**Čekaj!**
Watch out for cars.	**Pazi na auta/ samovoze.**

METRIC CONVERSIONS

26. METRIC CONVERSIONS

Temperature - Toplina
To convert Celsius into Fahrenheit, multiply the degree Celsius by 1.8 and add 32. To convert Fahrenheit into Celsius, subtract 32 from the degree Fahrenheit and divide by 1.8.

$100°$ C = $212°$ F
$38°$ C = $100°$ F
$36.9°$ C = $98.4°$ F (body temperature)
$0°$ C = $32°$ F (freezing)

Distance - Razdaljina
To convert miles into kilometers, divide the miles by 5 and multiply by eight. To convert kilometers into miles, divide the kilometers by 8 and multiply by 5.

1 inch = 2.24 centimeters   1 centimeter = .39 inches
1 meter = 3.28 feet
1 kilometer = 0 .675 miles
1 mile = 1609 meters

Weight/Volume - Težina/Volumen
1 kilogram = 2.2 pounds   1 liter = .264 gallons
1 pound = 453.6 grams   1 gallon = 3.8 liter
1 gram = .0325 ounces   1 liter = 1.06 quarts
1 ounce = 28.35 grams   1 quart = .95 liter